The Great Departure

❦ AMERICA IN CRISIS

A series of eight books on American Diplomatic History

EDITOR: *Robert A. Divine*

The Great Departure

The United States and World War I

1914–1920

DANIEL M. SMITH

Professor of History, University of Colorado

John Wiley and Sons, Inc., New York · London · Sydney

For Stephanie
Danny
and
Greg

Foreword

"THE UNITED STATES always wins the war and loses the peace," runs a persistent popular complaint. Neither part of the statement is accurate. The United States barely escaped the War of 1812 with its territory intact, and in Korea in the 1950's the nation was forced to settle for a stalemate on the battlefield. At Paris in 1782, and again in 1898, American negotiators drove hard bargains to win notable diplomatic victories. Yet the myth persists, along with the equally erroneous American belief that we are a peaceful people. Our history is studded with conflict and violence. From the Revolution to the Cold War, Americans have been willing to fight for their interests, their beliefs, and their ambitions. The United States has gone to war for many objectives — for independence in 1775, for honor and trade in 1812, for territory in 1846, for humanity and empire in 1898, for neutral rights in 1917, and for national security in 1941. Since 1945 the nation has been engaged in a deadly struggle to contain communism and defend the democratic way of life.

The purpose of this series is to examine in detail eight critical periods relating to American involvement in foreign war from the Revolution through the Cold War. Each author has set out to recount anew the breakdown of diplomacy that led to war and the subsequent quest for peace. The emphasis is on foreign policy, and no effort is made to chronicle the military participation of the United States in these wars. Instead the authors focus on the day-by-day conduct of diplomacy to explain why the nation went to war and to show how peace was restored. Each volume is a synthesis combining the research of other historians with new insights to provide a fresh interpretation of a critical period in

American diplomatic history. It is hoped that this series will help dispel the illusion of national innocence and give Americans a better appreciation of their country's role in war and peace.

ROBERT A. DIVINE

Preface

A MERICAN INVOLVEMENT in World War I signified, in the phrase of historian C. Vann Woodward, the passing of the Age of Free Security. In the nineteenth century the United States had been the fortunate beneficiary of a century of general peace in Europe and the usually benevolent role of British seapower. The resultant peace and prosperity, however, had been too often wrongly attributed to America's deliberate choice of an isolationist policy toward European politics. Thus President Grover Cleveland, in his inaugural address in 1885, assured his fellow citizens that: "The genius of our institutions, the needs of our people . . . dictate the scrupulous avoidance of any departure from that foreign policy commended by the history, the traditions, and the prosperity of the Republic. It is the policy of independence. . . . It is the policy of peace suitable to our interests. . . . It is the policy of neutrality, rejecting any share in foreign broils and ambitions upon other continents. . . ." [1] As Cleveland indicated, by the late nineteenth century American isolationism had come to mean not total separation from Europe, particularly in the cultural and economic areas, but political abstention from foreign wars and an adamant refusal to enter into alliances with other states. The years 1914 and especially 1917, however, revealed that the nation could not be isolated from the effects of a major world war and that, in contrast to the past, a much higher cost in manpower and money would have to be paid for national security in a turbulent age. Yet an

---

[1] James D. Richardson, ed., *A Compilation of the Messages and Papers of the Presidents, 1789–1897* (Washington, 1900), VIII, 301.

isolationist psychology was retained by most Americans and helps account for the subsequent popular disillusionment with America's participation in the war and the peacemaking. It was within such a climate that the great historical debate about the causes of the involvement raged in the 1920's and 1930's.

Two main questions are raised by study of this period: Why did the United States reluctantly depart from its traditions of neutrality to become a belligerent in 1917? And why did Americans, after entering the conflict and having decisively tipped the balance to ensure an Allied victory, reject the peace treaty which their own president had largely shaped and which presumably justified the sacrifices of the war? The fruits of victory were tossed aside, with the result that the United States tried to retire into an isolationist shell and to a large degree abandoned control over future world developments.

Although historians have not been able to agree on the answers to these questions, this brief study will try to offer one. Most Americans lacked an understanding of the basic reasons why the country entered the war and of the nation's specific stake in the peace settlement. The United States entered the war, in an involved controversy over neutral rights, because of national self-interests and an even greater concern in the creation of a stable and just postwar world society. American foreign policy, throughout the neutrality and the war periods, was in general practical and based on these national interests. Even the Wilsonian concept of an idealistic peace and a global collective security system was related to practical national interests. But the majority of citizens was not made fully aware of that fact and was too easily wearied by the responsibilities of world leadership. There lay the tragedy of America in World War I.

In a volume of this brevity on so large a topic, I have been compelled to be selective and interpretive rather than encyclopedic. Footnotes, except to acknowledge the source of quotations, have necessarily been omitted. In addition to my research in the relevant unpublished materials, the bibliographical essay on published books and articles indicates my indebtedness to the work of others. I am grateful to the Council on Research and Creative Work of the Graduate School of the University of

Colorado for a grant to complete this volume. And to my wife, Aladeen, for her careful typing and general encouragement is due my principal debt.

DANIEL M. SMITH

Boulder, Colo.
March 1965

Contents

MAPS

(Maps by Theodore R. Miller)

The Great Departure

CHAPTER I

The Shock of War

THE ERUPTION OF WAR in August of 1914 caused nearly universal disbelief and shock. Despite many indications of impending catastrophe in the preceding decade, at each crisis a major conflict had been narrowly averted. The two rival blocs, the Central Alliance of Germany, Austria-Hungary, and Italy versus the Triple Entente of France, Russia, and Great Britain, were locked in an arms race and competition for prestige. Yet many thoughtful people, inspired by nineteenth-century concepts of liberalism and free trade, believed that the modern world had outgrown war. Actual armed struggles between the major powers, the centers of civilization and industry, were viewed as almost impossible for the world presumably had so advanced morally and materially as to render a large-scale war anachronistic.

History buttressed that conviction, for there had been no general European war since the final defeat of Napoleon in 1815. Peace societies flourished, schemes for the peaceful adjustment of international conflict abounded, and the Hague conferences of 1899 and 1907 had apparently made progress toward the codification of international law and the creation of arbitration machinery. The optimism engendered by these developments was rudely shattered by the events of June–August in 1914: on June 28, in the comparatively remote Balkans, Archduke Franz Ferdinand, heir to the Austro-Hungarian throne, was assassinated by Slav nationalists at Sarajevo; attributing the deed to Serbian nationalists seeking to disrupt the empire, the Vienna government followed an ultimatum with a declaration of war against Serbia on July 28; resultant Russian and French mobilization quickly led to a German declaration of war against those two

1

allies, on August 1 and 3; and on August 4, after Germany invaded Belgium, Great Britain entered the struggle on the side of France and Russia. Ultimately, almost all of Europe was engulfed in the struggle, and in the Far East Japan, allied to Great Britain since 1902, also entered the war.

The general reaction to the war in the United States was one of horror and dismay mingled with a feeling of relief that America was immune from the insanity gripping the old world. The long-established tradition of abstention from Europe's politics and wars, and the barrier of the Atlantic moat, seemed to ensure that the United States would remain aloof. When President Woodrow Wilson formally proclaimed American neutrality and subsequently appealed for neutrality in thought and speech as well, most citizens reacted with complete approval. A *New York Sun* editorial summed up the general view: "There is nothing reasonable in such a war . . . and it would be folly for the country to sacrifice itself to the frenzy of dynastic policies and the clash of ancient hatreds which is urging the Old World to destruction." [1]

I

The impartiality in speech and thought requested by the president quickly proved impossible to attain. America was composed of too polyglot a population, with ethnic groups still emotionally involved in the old world lands of their origin. Of a population of nearly ninety-two million people in 1914, approximately one-third could be classified as "hyphenated" Americans, in the sense of being either foreign born or of having one or both parents as immigrants. German-Americans numbered over eight million and, judged by the attitudes of their newspapers and social organizations, they were inclined to be strongly sympathetic to the cause of the fatherland. To them, imperial Germany was waging a defensive war against the Slavic peril represented by czarist Russia. The Irish-Americans, over four million strong, embodied centuries of bitterness at English rule and tended to

---

[1] As quoted in *The Literary Digest*, 49:215–217 (August 8, 1914).

favor the cause of the Central Powers, as did most of the Russian-hating American Jewry. Conversely, most "native" or old-stock Americans were at least mildly pro-Entente in sentiment, the result of cultural, ethnic, and language bonds with Great Britain and of the traditional Franco-American friendship. Of equal importance, probably, was the Anglo-American *rapprochement* which had occurred at the turn of the century. During the same period, when major Anglo-American disputes over an isthmian canal and the Alaskan boundary with Canada were being settled to the satisfaction of the United States, German-American relations had experienced a slow deterioration. In large part this development merely reflected the parallel growth of the two latecomer great powers, with the virtually inevitable result of rivalry over markets and naval coaling stations. Suspicions and rivalry in Samoa and the Philippines, no doubt exaggerated, together with the unfortunate penchant of Germany's ruler, Kaiser Wilhelm II, for swashbuckling gestures, helped create an American image of imperial Germany as autocratic, militaristic, and expansionist.

Belligerent propaganda campaigns aimed at America began early in the war. Although the German effort has usually been evaluated as lagging far behind that of the Allies, recent studies reveal that it was by no means inept and ineffective. In August the German Information Service was established in New York City. Under the direction of Dr. Bernhard Dernburg, aided by Dr. Heinrich Albert and others, this agency issued news bulletins and distributed pamphlets and books which sought to justify Germany's actions and to place responsibility for the war on the Allied powers. French desires for revenge for the losses to Germany in 1870 and Russian expansionism were allegedly the causes of the conflict, whereas Germany fought to defend western civilization against the Slavic peril. But certain handicaps confronted German propaganda efforts in America. Most of the major newspapers were pro-Ally, so reliance had to be put on German and Irish journals. Cables to Europe either had been cut or were under Allied control. Although it was more difficult to get a flow of materials and news from Germany than it was from the Allies, much material got to America via indirect cable routes, by mail, and by wireless. Moreover, German propaganda activities were exposed and at least partly discredited by a series of disasters in the summer of 1915. First came the famed affair of Dr. Albert's briefcase, which he accidentally left behind him when debarking from a New York City elevated train; seized by an American secret service agent, the contents of the briefcase revealed the extent of German propaganda operations and created a sensation when released through the *New York World*. The affair was followed by the expulsion of the Austrian ambassador, Constantine Dumba, and subsequently of the German naval and military *attachés*, for diplomatic improprieties and violations of American neutrality. Despite such reverses, effective propaganda was continued through the embassy in Washington and its able head, Ambassador Johann von Bernstorff.

Great Britain naturally assumed chief responsibility for Allied propaganda activities in America. Although initially trailing the German efforts, British propaganda soon surpassed its rival in extensive organization and effectiveness. A centralized and secret propaganda ministry was established in Wellington House in London under the direction of Charles Masterman. It contained divisions for the principal belligerent and neutral countries, and sought to maintain a careful scrutiny of public opinion abroad and to tailor propaganda accordingly. The American section was in the charge of Sir Gilbert Parker, well known to many prominent Americans. Parker's staff conducted weekly surveys of the American press, compiled mailing lists of influential Americans and organizations, and sent to these a stream of materials skillfully designed to appeal to various ethnic, religious, and social groups.

British propaganda utilized to good effect alleged German atrocities in northern France and Belgium and such incidents as the execution of Nurse Edith Cavell as a spy in 1915. In May of that year, Lord Bryce released a report which contained numerous depositions and accounts charging deliberate German violations of the rules of warfare. Supposedly an objective documentation of atrocities, endorsed by well-known scholars, the report contained much second- or thirdhand testimony by unnamed witnesses and the accounts fell into the stereotyped categories familiar in other wars. Although such stories, especially the Bryce Report, undoubtedly affected many Americans, the general propaganda themes that German aggression alone was responsible for the war and that the Allies were fighting in defense of civilization against ruthless militaristic and authoritarian opponents were far more effective in molding opinion. Allied propaganda also benefited enormously from the obvious fact that Germany had violated Belgian neutrality and that the war in the west was being fought against German invaders on Allied soil. Germany also experimented with new forms of warfare, which probably were not essentially more inhuman than the usual practices but which aroused widespread shock and condemnation: dirigible bombardment of cities, poison gas barrages, and submerged submarine attacks against enemy merchant and passenger vessels. These novel weapons, unsanctioned by past usage, made it far easier to portray Germany's masters as brutal and utterly ruthless.

It is difficult to measure accurately the effects of belligerent propaganda in America. Writers in the 1930's tended to exaggerate the impact of Allied propaganda and to attribute the subsequent involvement of the United States in the war to its success. Atrocity stories and ideological appeals presumably explained how neutral America was pulled into the great struggle. Later historians have found that explanation too simple and largely unsubstantiated. Propaganda was extensive, and probably had some effect in strengthening the pro-Ally sentiments held by most Americans — to that extent America was more prone to accept Allied control of the seas while objecting to the German submarine challenge. British propaganda thus scored some success in persuading Americans to accept the Allied blockade and in strengthening wartime economic bonds. Yet it was partially offset by German propaganda efforts, at least until late in the neutrality period. Furthermore, most Americans appear to have formed their basic attitudes toward the war before extensive propaganda could be launched by either belligerent. And finally, although most Americans were at least mildly pro-Ally in sentiment, the great majority obviously believed neutrality was the wisest course and were reluctant to enter the war until early in 1917.

II

The European war also gave a severe shock to the American economy. A recession had been underway prior to August 1914, and the outbreak of hostilities at first caused a further deterioration. International exchanges were disrupted, stock market prices tumbled, the cotton market nearly collapsed with the threatened loss of the German and Austrian market, and many European investors liquidated their American holdings. Thousands of frantic citizens were stranded in Europe, temporarily bereft of credit and with their relatives in America bombarding officials with inquiries as to their safety. American export trade with Europe, in large part dependent on British and other foreign shipping, was adversely affected. The Wilson administration reacted with speed to cushion the impact of war, adopting measures ranging from the issuance of special credits to citizens stranded in Europe to use of emergency currency at home.

Within a short time the economy began to adjust to the war and under the impetus of Allied war purchases recovered from the recession and began an upward spiral of prosperity. War orders flooded in for foodstuffs, raw materials, and munitions. American production of iron, steel, copper, oil, meat, wheat, and other materials was vastly increased and the value of exports to Europe steadily mounted. Despite the virtual loss of the German market and Allied controls over European neutral imports, American exports to Europe rose from an excess over imports of 500 million dollars in 1914 to three and a half billion in 1917. Trade with the Allies increased 184 per cent over peacetime. A virtually new munitions industry was created by Allied purchases, and by 1917 America had exported over one billion dollars' worth of explosives and arms to Europe.

In view of these facts, it was not surprising that many citizens and scholars in the 1930's, disillusioned by the war and affected by the sensational Nye Committee investigation of the munitions industry, concluded that the country had been pulled into World War I by the golden chain of economic forces. It was alleged that the one-sided American war trade with the Allies and the vast loans of money had made the United States a silent member of the Allied camp. Involvement in the war had been the inevitable result, since an enraged Germany had been driven to ruthless U-boat warfare in order to halt the burgeoning flow of war supplies to its enemies. Some also suggested that the United States had entered the fray as an active belligerent in order to prevent an Allied defeat and the consequent loss of American loans. Little evidence exists to substantiate these interpretations. Although the Wilson administration was seriously concerned with the health of the American economy and defended the war trade as legitimate, it never contemplated hostilities to ensure continued prosperity or to protect the American stake in the Allies. Most citizens and high officials in the government were confident throughout the neutrality period that the Allied powers would eventually triumph over Germany. In any case, the majority of the loans to the Allies were amply secured by pledged collateral, regardless of the outcome of the war. And as for Germany's adoption of unrestricted submarine warfare, the evidence reveals conclusively that the motive was not merely to sever the war trade between America and England but was to cut off all trade with the British Isles and to starve that nation into submission.

CHAPTER II

American Interests and the World War

IN RECENT YEARS historians have examined closely the role of national self-interest in propelling the United States into World War I. For two decades after that war ended, the scholarly debate was centered on the question of whether the country had been genuinely neutral in 1914–1917, with the defenders of the Wilson administration contending that hostilities had resulted only because of German submarine attacks on American rights and lives on the high seas, while critics ("revisionists") attributed involvement to the administration's allegedly unneutral policies favoring the Allied cause. The coming of World War II, when the Axis powers posed a manifest threat to American security and national values, suggested the need for a reevaluation of the causes of the earlier struggle. Wartime books, like Walter Lippmann's *U. S. Foreign Policy: Shield of the Republic*, reinterpreted the decision for war in 1917 as necessitated by the German challenge to Anglo-American control of the north Atlantic and to the security of the United States in the Western Hemisphere. A decisive German victory would have supplanted British with German naval power and would have constituted a real and immediate danger to North America. Since 1945 a number of scholars have reexamined President Wilson's foreign policies and have inquired into the role of considerations of the national economic and security interests in the decision for war. The answers reveal that realistic concepts of the national interests were held by Wilson and his principal advisers and were involved to a degree in the formulation of basic neutrality policies and the ultimate transition to belligerency.

I

In the years after the Spanish-American War, a number of influential Americans began to view Germany as a dynamic and imperialistic power potentially dangerous to the United States. Both countries were relatively new to the ranks of great world powers, and were rapidly industrializing and seeking overseas markets and coaling stations. A measure of rivalry was virtually inescapable. During the war with Spain, the German government had indicated a definite interest in acquiring a share of the Philippine Islands in case the United States relinquished them, and the conduct of the German naval squadron observing American military operations in Manila Bay gave rise to a legend of a hostile plot to intervene in Spain's behalf. After the brief war, some American naval and army officers were convinced that German economic and territorial ambitions constituted a threat to the nation's security and its hegemony in Latin America. The Navy General Board in 1901 emphasized the imperative necessity of controlling the Caribbean Sea and the approaches to the Panama Canal, and opposed acquisition of territory in the area by any foreign power as a menace to American security. The Board recommended purchase of the Danish West Indies, since "In view of the isthmian canal and the German settlements in South America, every additional acquisition by the United States in the West Indies is of value." [1] Rumors of alleged German attempts to acquire naval bases in the Galapagos Islands and in Haiti brought repeated objections by the military departments to the State Department in 1910–1912. The vital Panama Canal, nearing completion, would be endangered by such foreign lodgments.

During these years, naval planners contended that Germany and Japan offered the most serious potential danger to American interests. The navy, therefore, should be sufficiently enlarged to cope with all eventualities. The Navy League of the United

---

[1] General Board No. 187, Report of November 12, 1901, Naval War Records Office (Arlington, Virginia).

States, founded by civilian enthusiasts in 1902 with Navy Department approval and patterned after European organizations, clamored for a larger navy to cope with threats to the Monroe Doctrine. Germany was viewed as the principal challenger of that sacred national policy and the press releases of the Navy League pointed out the ominous portents of American naval inferiority to the Kaiser's fleets. Although its efforts were only moderately successful, a recurrent theme of the League's publications prior to 1914 was the possible German menace to American security. The Navy General Board concurred and a confidential estimate in 1910 depicted Germany as thwarted in its expansionist drives both in the Pacific and in Latin America: "it is seen that there are latent causes that render a break with Germany more probable than with either of the other two great maritime powers. . . ." [2] The War Department shared these views and drafted plans for repelling a German attack on North America. A War College paper in 1909–1910 described Germany as surpassing the United States in many areas of economic competition in Latin America and the Far East and as colonizing extensively in Brazil in an apparently well-planned move. Because France and Great Britain had preempted most of Africa and the United States had blocked expansion in the Far East and Latin America, the author of the paper concluded that "while war may never result between the United States and Germany yet the student of history must recognize the existence of causes [economic] which tend to produce it. . . ." [3]

Apprehension of Germany existed outside military circles. A. T. Mahan, advocate of naval expansion, published books and articles on America's interest in seapower and in the world balance of power. Theodore Roosevelt and members of his circle were greatly influenced by Mahan's realistic appraisals of world politics and his emphasis on an Anglo-American community of interest. Roosevelt wrote his friend Henry Cabot Lodge in 1901

---

[2] War Portfolio No. 1, Atlantic Station—approved by the Navy General Board, October 19, 1910, Naval War Records Office, and recirculated in 1915.

[3] "The Military Geography of the Atlantic Seaboard . . ." by Captain Paul B. Malone, War College Division, General Staff, 6916-1, War Materials Division, National Archives.

that only Germany might be "a menace to us in anything like the immediate future," whereas "we are closer to her [England] than to any other nation; and . . . probably her interest and ours will run on rather parallel lines in the future." [4] His friends Henry and Brooks Adams concurred that Anglo-American interests coincided, with the United States probably destined eventually to assume the leadership as British power slowly deteriorated.

Other informed citizens also began to view Germany as a potential enemy, while envisioning Great Britain with its sea power as fulfilling a benevolent and protective role. The editors of the *New York Times*, after 1898, advocated closer ties with England as the one great power that shared a community of interests with America, and they called for at least naval parity with Germany. American periodicals from time to time carried articles expressing great distrust of German ambitions as they affected the Western Hemisphere. Comparisons of the German and American navies were occasionally made. *Munsey's Magazine* in 1901 recommended increased naval construction and cooperation with Great Britain to meet the German challenge to the new world.

Articles from English journals on the same themes were reprinted in American periodicals. One of the most prophetic essays was written by an Indiana University professor of political science, Amos S. Hershey, in 1909 for *The Independent*. Professor Hershey depicted Germany as endangering both world peace and American economic and security interests, and he urged that the menace be countered by the formation of an Anglo-American alliance. If an Anglo-German war should occur, he predicted that America could hardly remain neutral if Germany seemed about to triumph and to wrest naval supremacy from Great Britain: "A blockade of the British Isles by German cruisers and submarine mines, or the loss involved in the dangers to contraband trade would be severely felt in

---

[4] Roosevelt to Lodge, March 27 and June 19, 1901, *Selections from the Correspondence of Theodore Roosevelt and Henry Cabot Lodge* (New York: Scribner, 1925, 2 vols.), I, 484–486, 493–494.

this country."[5] Writing in the same year, the well-known English commentator Sydney Brooks noted that a growing number of Americans were aware that isolationism was no longer feasible and that Germany was as much an American as a British problem. In a war between England and Germany, he concluded that the United States would be benevolently neutral toward the British cause and might enter the struggle if Germany threatened to halt the export of American foodstuffs to the British Isles. On the eve of the great war, the American career diplomat Lewis Einstein joined this small group of writers in emphasizing the importance to the United States of a friendly British naval power and the dangers that would ensue if Germany achieved naval supremacy. In an article entitled "The United States and Anglo-German Rivalry," published anonymously in Britain in 1913, Einstein examined the probable results of a German victory, which he believed would affect adversely American economic and political interests in the Caribbean and the Far East. He predicted that the United States might find it necessary to intervene in order to prevent a British defeat and the consequent creation of an unfavorable balance of power.

The outbreak of war in 1914 enhanced the belief of a number of citizens that the national interest required an Allied victory. Editorials and letters in the *New York Times,* and several articles by historians George Louis Beer, George Burton Adams, and Albert Bushnell Hart, contended that security and maintenance of the Monroe Doctrine required the preservation of British naval supremacy. To Beer, "German ambitions in South America have been dormant only because the British fleet was an insuperable barrier. . . . Similar dangers threaten our economic interests in the Far East."[6] Hart pointed out the nation's stake in the existing world equipoise, which affected the country's ability to defend the Monroe Doctrine: "Peace can be

[5] Amos S. Hershey, "Germany—the Main Obstacle to the World's Peace," *The Independent,* 66:1071–1076 (May 20, 1909).

[6] George Louis Beer, "America's Part Among the Nations," *New Republic,* 5:62–64 (November 20, 1915).

maintained only by convincing Germany and Japan, which are the two Powers most likely to be moved by an ambition to possess American territory." [7] To Adams, apart from valid idealistic and ideological factors, "political and military expediency" justified intervention to preclude a German triumph over the Allies.[8] A sweeping German success would leave no power in Europe able to restrain its ambitions; the United States at the minimum would have to exist in a hostile world as a result and probably would face direct Teutonic challenges. Other well-known scholars and commentators, such as Walter Lippmann of the *New Republic,* presented papers on these themes at the 1916 assembly of the American Academy of Political and Social Science. Books and articles by H. H. Powers, Roland G. Usher, and Hudson Maxim also warned of the dangers of a German victory.

The great majority of Americans, however, were not accustomed to the contemplation of foreign policy based on realistic appraisals of economic and political interests. Instead, popular reactions in 1914–1917 largely reflected traditional isolationist attitudes, modified by some emotional and ideological sympathy with the Allies. It is clear, nevertheless, that for over a decade a minority of informed citizens had been exposed to repeated warnings that an aggressive Germany potentially endangered an Anglo-American community of interests. They had come to view Great Britain as the bulwark standing between the Western Hemisphere and Europe, whose removal would expose the United States to great peril. Such views were particularly prevalent in the eastern part of the United States, and were held by people with considerable influence in the molding of public opinion. Existence of these attitudes and convictions made it inestimably easier to condemn Germany on moral and idealistic grounds and probably facilitated the ultimate entry into war.

---

[7] Albert Bushnell Hart, "Shall We Defend the Monroe Doctrine?," *The North American Review,* 202:681–692 (November 1915).

[8] George Burton Adams, "America's Obligation and Opportunity," *Yale Review,* V (1915-1916), 474–483.

II

The most influential advisers of President Wilson shared a "realistic" appraisal of the significance of the European war for the United States. Robert Lansing, counselor of the State Department and its second in command, presidential adviser Edward M. House, and ambassadors Walter Hines Page in London and James W. Gerard in Berlin, together with several cabinet members, fused pro-Ally sentiments and ideological considerations with apprehensions that a German victory would affect adversely American economic and political interests. These views, however, were most emphatically not held by William Jennings Bryan, Wilson's first secretary of state.

Three times the Democratic candidate for the presidency, Bryan had a large and devoted popular following and expediency had caused President Wilson to appoint him to the State Department in 1913. From every point of view except politics, he was manifestly a poor choice. The "Great Commoner" was indelibly stamped with rural populism and was a dangerous if ludicrous figure to the educated and "respectable" classes, especially in the urban and eastern areas of the country. Unquestionably, he was one of the most unsophisticated secretaries of state in the history of the republic. His frank spoilsmanship in appointments to the foreign service, the substitution of grape juice and carbonated water for alcoholic beverages at formal dinners, continued paid lecturing on the Chautauqua circuit, and his homey habits and expressions offered the hostile press ample opportunity for savagely satirical comment.

Bryan was a near-pacifist. Influenced by biblical injunctions and by the example of the Russian Count Tolstoy, he believed that moral force, reason, and Christian love would inevitably triumph over physical force. Long before he entered the sedate halls of the State Department, Bryan had opposed a large army and navy for the United States as undesirable additions to the current global arms race. He lacked the capacity to survey world relations realistically and to compute the national course in accordance with its material interests, ideals, and power. A world tour in 1905-1906 had done little to broaden his horizons; it could be safely said that in a very real sense he had never left home. Everywhere he saw countries and events through the wrong-ended telescope of his own naive predilections, and he returned to America apparently little wiser than he had left. The yardstick which he applied to the world was that of the Christian and progressive United States, the moral exemplar of all mankind, and he was confident that American ideals and values commanded respect abroad and would eventually enjoy universal acknowledgment.

As secretary of state, Bryan, like Wilson, was determined to use the nation's influence for good in world affairs. Historian Arthur S. Link* has aptly described their approach as a "missionary diplomacy" of moral exhortation and example. Bryan was especially interested in the cause of world peace. In addition to supplementing previous arbitration treaties with thirty "cooling-off" pacts, designed to resolve crises through investigation and delay, he repeatedly pledged the American people that the nation would not become involved in war while he was in charge of the State Department.

Bryan had less of a policy and more of an emotional reaction toward the European war. He took a firmly moral view of American neutrality from the first days of the conflict. Deeply shocked by the carnage and without concern for the practical portents of the war, he saw no danger to the United States if Germany emerged the master of Europe. After one conversation on the subject with Bryan, House noted with near incredulity that the secretary "did not believe there was the slightest danger to this country from foreign invasion, even if the Germans were successful. . . . He talked as innocently as my little grandchild. . . ." [9] Bryan viewed the war as merely a temporary reversal in the universal march toward peace and he was passionately convinced that the role for the United States should

---

* For this and other unfootnoted references to historians, consult their works listed in the bibliography.

[9] November 8, 1914, House Diary, The Papers of Edward M. House, Yale University Library.

be to restore sanity by remaining neutral and mediating the struggle. America, he believed, was the foremost Christian spokesman for democracy, which would ultimately bring peace and progress to all peoples. The nation, therefore, must offer a moral example to the world.

The secretary was untiring in his advocacy of mediation. He hailed Wilson's formal tender of good offices in August 1914 in biblical language: "He has sent the dove out of the ark in search of dry land — God speed its return with the olive leaf." [10] Repeatedly Bryan called Wilson's attention to the possibilities of further peace efforts. At his suggestion, October 4, 1914, was designated as a national day of prayer for peace. In a moving address in New York City on the proclaimed day, Bryan emphasized the economic interdependence of all nations and asserted that a peace based on territorial aggrandizement and a continued arms race could not long endure. Reflecting the current concepts of the peace movement, the secretary argued to Wilson that the most desirable peace settlement would be one that reduced armaments to the level of mere national police forces, with a mutual pledge by the nations to respect the territorial integrity of others. This vision of an ideal peace appealed strongly to the president but he judged the time inopportune for a renewed effort at mediation. Acting upon House's advice that the Allies would probably reject any overture while the military situation strongly favored Germany, Wilson reluctantly declined to act.

Unlike many Americans, Bryan was not persuaded that Germany alone was responsible for the initiation of hostilities. In any case, he was less interested in distributing guilt for the outbreak of war and more in determining the responsibility for continuation of the struggle. From that point of view he held the Allies to be equally as selfish as the Central powers. It would be better, therefore, for America not to wait until the Allied states had won enough victories to restore the military balance before making a strong peace effort. The holocaust, he argued, should be ended by immediate efforts toward a restoration of peace. Wilson and House, however, were then convinced not only that untimely overtures for mediation would be fore-

---

[10] August 1914, *The Commoner.*

doomed but that it was unwise from the American viewpoint to embarrass the Allies while Germany held the upper hand and would emerge with the largest gains. Such considerations of expediency and interests left Bryan unaffected. Peace, whatever its dimensions, was his sole aim.

III

Robert Lansing, the counselor of the State Department, held diametrically opposed views of the war. A descendant of a distinguished New York family and trained in international law, Lansing had traveled extensively abroad and by 1914 had participated in more international arbitrations than probably any other living American. As a result of training and experience, he was eminently practical and "hard-headed" in his approach to world affairs and questions of foreign policy. Although he shared the American faith in the efficacy and future of democracy and as a devout Presbyterian believed in the moral imperative, Lansing recognized that amoral physical power was the underlying reality in international relations. Moral law did and should govern domestic society, but unfortunately relations between states were characterized by materialistic and selfish motives and conflicts usually were resolved by violence. In essence a nation dealt with other nations in a savage manner, regardless of how enlightened the conduct of its domestic affairs might be. To assume otherwise, to believe that foreign policy should be founded solely on altruistic motives, was fallacious and a grave error. Idealism had an important place in American foreign policy but it needed to be harmonized with common sense.

The initial response of Lansing to the war was one of relief that his country was spared the waste and sufferings of the conflict. Yet he was pro-Ally from the first, in part because of emotional and cultural attachments to Great Britain, and in part because of his conviction that the Allies represented the democratic impulse against the aggressive autocracy of the Central powers. He assumed, as many others, that the war would soon end in an Allied triumph, and at first he concentrated on perfecting American neutrality. By early 1915, however, he perceived that the war would be a long and bitter one seriously affecting the economic and political interests of the United States. Submarine warfare, a novel and rude challenge to trade and past international practices, seemed to Lansing to portend a possible German victory. The destruction of British passenger liners with American travelers aboard removed all doubt from his mind and underscored America's interest in the outcome of the war. Germany, he believed, was a very real danger to American ideals and to its economic interests and security.

On July 11, 1915, a few days after he had succeeded Bryan as secretary of state, Lansing recorded in his private notebook his views on policy:

I have come to the conclusion that the German Government is utterly hostile to all nations with democratic institutions because those who compose it see in democracy a menace to absolutism and the defeat of the German ambition for world domination. Everywhere German agents are plotting and intriguing to accomplish the supreme purpose of their Government. . . . Germany must not be permitted to win this war and to break even, though to prevent it this country is forced to take an active part. This ultimate necessity must be constantly in our minds in all our controversies with the belligerents. . . ."

If Germany should win, the United States would be confronted with a hostile naval power threatening its interests in the Caribbean, in Latin America generally, and perhaps in the Far East as well. The United States had already experienced sharp controversies with an expansionist Japan, frequently rumored to be on the verge of deserting the Allies and realigning with the Central powers. Lansing could envision, therefore, the possibility of a future grand alliance between the three autocratic empires of Germany, Russia, and Japan, which would isolate the United States in a menacing world.

The new secretary was also imbued with the American faith in democracy and its eventual universal triumph. Democratic states were inherently peace-loving, he believed, because the ordinary citizen presumably never desires war and its costly sacrifices, which fall heaviest on the average man, whereas auto-

---

¹¹ July 11, 1915, Private Memoranda, The Papers of Robert Lansing, Library of Congress.

cratic states with dynastic rivalries were basically aggressive and militaristic. From the point of view of Lansing and others similarly inclined, imperial Germany, the leading representative of a militaristic and statist philosophy, could be said to be a triple threat to the United States: ideologically it menaced democratic institutions and values, militarily it endangered the nation's security, and it was the most serious rival of the United States for economic and political influence in Latin America. To cope with these dangers, Lansing resolved to endeavor to watch carefully German activity in Latin America, especially in turbulent Mexico and the Caribbean area, to take steps to forestall possible German acquisition of bases by American purchase of the Danish West Indies (done in 1916–1917), to keep the submarine issue clearly defined, and to enter the war if it became necessary to avert a Teutonic victory.

Although ideological factors figured prominently in Lansing's thought, at least as important were considerations of the country's economic and security needs. In his private memoranda he repeatedly recorded the conviction that a German conquest in Europe would dangerously expose the United States. On the eve of America's entry into the war, he wrote: "The Allies must *not* be beaten. It would mean the triumph of Autocracy over Democracy; the shattering of all our moral standards; and a real, though it may seem remote, peril to our independence and institutions." [12] In 1915–1916, however, he appreciated the fact that public opinion was divided, with pacifist and isolationist traditions still strong, and that the president was most reluctant to contemplate actual hostilities. Insofar as he was able, therefore, he tried to shape the American course so that dangerous disputes with the Allies would be avoided, while the submarine issue was clearly delineated and the American people were slowly prepared by events for the great leap into belligerency. Lansing usually did not speak to Wilson directly of his belief that the nation's vital self-interests required preparation for war, but with an understanding of the presidential psychology he instead used moralistic and legalistic arguments to justify what he viewed as the correct policy. Often working in close

---

[12] January 28, 1917, Lansing Private Memoranda.

cooperation with the similarly inclined Colonel House, Lansing was able to achieve a large measure of influence on Wilsonian foreign policy.

Other officials within the State Department and the foreign service held comparable views on the meaning of the war. James Brown Scott, William Phillips, and Frank L. Polk (later undersecretary) were also pro-Ally in sympathies and were persuaded that a German triumph would endanger America. Chandler P. Anderson, a legal adviser on problems of neutrality, remarked after a discussion with Lansing of a recent German note that it was surly in tone and "a good example of the sort of lecturing and regulating that all nations might expect if Germany succeeded in its ambition to rule the world." [13] From London, Ambassador Walter Hines Page sought to convince Wilson and top administration figures that Britain's fight against Germany was in the best interests of the United States. Only if the Allies won, he wrote, would a favorable power balance be preserved in the Far East and in the Atlantic. Ambassador James W. Gerard in Berlin had similar apprehensions and predicted that if the Central powers emerged victorious "we are next on their list. . . ." [14]

IV

Edward M. House of Texas, usually referred to by his honorary title of colonel (which he disliked), is generally conceded to have had the greatest individual influence on President Wilson's domestic and foreign policies. Born into a wealthy Texas family, young House had been frail of health but intensely ambitious and he early turned to politics as his *metier*. Confining his role to that of a behind-the-scenes manipulator, he helped direct several successful campaigns in his native state before applying his talents to the national stage. He attached

---

[13] April 8, 1915, Anderson Diary, The Papers of Chandler P. Anderson, Library of Congress.
[14] Gerard to Lansing, October 25, 1915, *Papers Relating to the Foreign Relations of the United States: The Lansing Papers, 1914-1920* (Washington, 1940, 2 vols.), I, 675–676.

himself to Wilson's cause in 1912 and speedily became the intimate friend and counselor of the professor in politics. A very intelligent and able man, House asked no political office for himself and desired only the role of a privy counselor. He understood well the psychology of the new president and sought to influence him by quiet suggestion and indirect recommendations. House avoided arguing with Wilson and usually lapsed into silence when he strongly disagreed with some action or view. For reasons of health, and apparently because he realized it was the wisest approach, he continued to live in New York City during the Wilson administration and maintained contact with the president through letters, telephone conversations, and occasional visits. He also relied upon certain administration officials to keep him informed of developments and *au courant* with presidential thinking. As a result, Wilson viewed House as a selfless and devoted friend upon whom he could depend for counsel and encouragement. So close was the relationship that Wilson referred to House as his second personality, whose thought almost automatically coincided with his own. Time was to reveal some pronounced divergencies but until the Paris Peace Conference the friendship flourished. House's ambition was to make an impression on history, but it was selfless in the sense that he desired to do so by making the administration of his friend preeminently successful in all areas. Some writers have been inclined to exaggerate his role and to attribute to House most of Wilson's notable achievements. Perhaps House's biographer, Charles Seymour, described his role more accurately when he depicted the colonel not as the master strategist but rather as the expediter and tactician who linked the recluse in the White House with the outside world.

Although lacking experience in foreign affairs prior to 1913, House had given some thought to the most desirable general policies for the United States. In his utopian novel *Philip Dru*, published anonymously in 1912, he sketched a foreign policy based on a world system of spheres of influence and a balance of power, with the United States playing a much larger role in the Western Hemisphere. He also expressed distrust of Russia and the hope that Japan would curb that nation in the Far East. House traveled to Europe in the summer of 1913 and established a close relationship with British Foreign Secretary Sir Edward Grey and other English leaders. In the months thereafter he planned another trip, on what he called his "Great Adventure," to "bring about an understanding between France, Germany, England, and the United States regarding a reduction of armaments . . ." and the development of backward areas of the world.[15] He was in Europe on this mission, with Wilson's encouragement, when the events occurred that plunged the world into the great war.

The 1914 trip and subsequent journeys not only familiarized House with the principal belligerent leaders but did much to convince him that the German government represented unrestrained militarism threatening the peace and welfare of the world. As a consequence he shared Lansing's views on the political and ideological connotations of the war. He differed, however, in that Lansing soon came to believe that only a decisive German defeat would suffice, whereas House long preferred a more limited Allied victory which would preserve the existing equipoise and leave Germany sufficiently strong to check the equally dangerous expansionist tendencies of czarist Russia. Consequently he later urged Wilson to undertake a form of mediation-intervention, but by early 1917 he had come to support active American involvement and the defeat of Germany.

In the early months of the war, House advised a benevolent neutrality of acquiescence in the Allied system of maritime warfare. With the advent of the U-boat issue, he joined Lansing in recommending a strong policy of opposition even at the risk of war. In the fall of 1915, House and Lansing conferred at length on foreign policy problems and agreed that the Allies should be reassured that "we considered their cause our cause, and that we had no intention of permitting a military autocracy [to] dominate the world if our strength would prevent it." [16] House, like Lansing, was fully aware that American neutrality favored the Allied cause, and he once complained to French Ambassador

---

[15] As quoted in Billie Barnes Jensen, "House, Wilson and American Neutrality, 1914–1917" (unpublished Ph.D. thesis, University of Colorado, 1962), 67.
[16] November 28, 1915, House Diary.

Jules Jusserand that "The United States had practiced benevolent neutrality toward the Allies which the Allies in no way appreciated." [17] As issues with Germany became clearly insoluble and after the failure of his own efforts at mediation-intervention, House cooperated with Secretary Lansing in support of a firmer stand toward Berlin and entry into the war.

V

President Wilson entered office surprisingly uninformed about foreign affairs. What was striking about this was not its novelty, since most presidents after the Civil War had been similarly ill-equipped, but was, as Arthur Link has pointed out, that it should have been true of Wilson, a professional historian and political scientist, author of a number of books and former president of Princeton University. Yet his publications indicated little interest in foreign affairs, and prior to 1898 he had written of diplomatic problems and machinery as almost a minor aspect of government. After the "passing" of the frontier and the Spanish-American War, he like others was made aware that the isolation of the nineteenth century was no longer possible and that the nation would perforce play an ever larger role in world affairs. Nothing indicated, however, that his knowledge and interest in international relations was more than perfunctory and superficial. In an oft-quoted remark, on the eve of his presidential inauguration, Wilson confessed to a friend that his primary interests were in domestic reform and that it would be "the irony of fate" if he should be compelled to concentrate on foreign affairs.

Wilson has been described by many scholars as primarily an idealist unresponsive to practical considerations in foreign relations and as unusually independent of his pro-Ally advisers in shaping America's course during the great war. Later studies have substantially modified such estimates. He was deeply moralistic in his approach, the result of being steeped in Calvinistic piety and training during his youth. Idealism usually meant for

---

[17] December 3, 1916, *ibid.*

him, however, not the ignoring of practical considerations but the exalting of noble purposes and goals. He has been aptly described as a "romantic moralist, who . . . raised every issue and conflict to a high stage. . . ." [18] He was capable of sometimes being blinded to reality by his faith and goals, as was painfully clear after the 1919 peace conference, but in the neutrality period his moralistic impulses usually were reenforced rather than contradicted by practical considerations of the national interest. Recent historians have revealed also that Wilson was by no means impervious to the counsel of his close advisers and that he shared to a degree their analyses of the meaning of the war to America's economic, security, and ideological interests.

When the war began, Wilson's first reactions were based on emotional sympathy for England and its allies, and he tended to attribute to Germany primary responsibility for beginning the struggle. Within a few months, however, he had recovered emotional balance and had come to realize that the causes of the war were complex and that guilt was more evenly distributed than he had at first suspected. Yet he remained sympathetic toward the Allies, especially Great Britain and its leaders in whom he had much trust and whom he long believed were pursuing more reasonable goals than were the other belligerents. He also came to appreciate the view that a decisive German victory would pose some danger for the United States. He indicated agreement with House that "if Germany won it would change the course of our civilization and make the United States a military nation." [19] Later in the fall of 1914, he told his private secretary Joseph Tumulty, that he would not pressure England to a dangerous point on the issue of neutral rights because Britain was fighting for the life of the world. During the *Arabic* crisis in mid-1915, he surprised House by stating that he had never been certain that America would not have to intervene in order to prevent a German victory. In 1916, in an effort to promote greater defensive military preparedness, Wilson repeatedly revealed in his public addresses serious concern for the national

---

[18] Arthur S. Link, "Woodrow Wilson: The Philosophy, Methods, and Impact of Leadership," in A. P. Dudden, ed., *Woodrow Wilson and the World of Today* (Philadelphia: University of Pennsylvania, 1957), 10.

[19] August 30, 1914, House Diary.

security and the long-range safety of Latin America. In these speeches he justified heavier expenditures on the army and navy as necessitated in part to protect American trade on the high seas and to avert possible dangers to the Western Hemisphere. Thus at Pittsburgh he asked rhetorically:

What is it that we want to defend? . . . We want to defend the life of this Nation against any sort of interference. We want to maintain the equal right of this Nation as against the action of all other nations, and we wish to maintain the peace and unity of the Western Hemisphere.[20]

Again, at Cleveland, he warned his audience that the United States "must play her part in keeping this conflagration from spreading to the people of the United States; she must also keep this conflagration from spreading on this side of the sea. These are matters in which our very life and our whole pride are embedded. . . ."[21]

It must be emphasized, however, that in general Wilson did not believe that a German victory, undesirable though it would be, would pose an immediate threat to the United States. Like most of his fellow citizens, he was confident of an eventual Allied triumph. But if the opposite should result, he thought that Germany probably would be too weakened by the European war to offer more than a future menace to the security of the Western Hemisphere. He remarked to a sceptical Colonel House, in late 1914, that Germany would need at least several years for recuperation before it could undertake a direct challenge to the United States. He adopted policies, therefore, which protected those national interests that were immediately affected by the war (commerce, legal rights, and prestige), and relied upon such measures as purchase of the Danish West Indies and increased military preparations to ward off future dangers to the national security and to the Monroe Doctrine. He was long convinced, in fact, that neutrality was the wisest course for America and that peace without victory for either belligerent side would alone make possible a just and stable postwar world.

---

[20] January 29, 1916, *President Wilson's State Papers and Addresses* (New York: Review of Reviews Co., 1917), 162–163.
[21] January 29, 1916, *Wilson's State Papers and Addresses*, 168–169.

The mission of the United States, therefore, was to stand as a bastion of liberty and peace, and to serve all mankind by helping to mediate this terrible struggle whenever events proved favorable. Not until early 1917, after the failure of his two peace overtures and the renewal of submarine warfare, did he accept the necessity for intervention in the war.

CHAPTER III

Trade and Blockade

THE ESSENTIAL CHARACTERISTICS of American neutrality emerged in the early months of the European war. International law and neutral obligations generally were interpreted in a manner favorable toward the Entente powers and specific policies were adopted which proved of benefit to that side: the munitions trade, credits and loans to the belligerents, and acquiescence in the British blockade of the Central powers. In contrast, the American government was to follow a more rigid course toward Germany's use of the submarine and to demand of that country full and immediate compliance with international law as interpreted by the United States. In fact, though theoretically impartial, American neutrality by mid-1915 operated strongly in favor of the Allies and had lost much of its appeal and value to Germany. Bonds of mutual interest and sentiment drew the United States closer to Great Britain and France, whereas little existed to moderate German-American relations.

The benevolence of American policies toward the Entente cause was apparently unplanned and virtually inescapable. Normal economic connections with England were quickened by war and the need of the Allies to purchase larger quantities of foodstuffs, raw materials, and munitions. Since the British Navy controlled the seas, at least the surface, the Allies alone had continuous access to the American market. President Wilson and his advisers were fully aware of the importance of the war trade to the American economy. In addition, House and Lansing, and Wilson to a degree, believed that the Allied leaders were more reasonable and trustworthy than their opponents and that American economic and political interests would be served if the Entente powers could avoid defeat. An important contributing factor was the determination of Sir Edward Grey, the British foreign secretary, to retain Anglo-American friendship despite the exigencies of war (because of British seapower, American controversies with the Allies were focused on Great Britain). Grey realized the imperative necessity of preserving good relations and in the early months of the war he persuaded his cabinet colleagues to follow as conciliatory a course as necessary to that end. The British government very gradually tightened the screws of economic warfare against Germany in order to cushion the blow to American trade, while Grey managed the diplomatic dialogue with Washington in a reasonable and accommodating manner. Eventually, the necessities of war and mounting political and popular pressures for a drastic blockade of the enemy compelled Grey to acquiesce in more vigorous measures affecting neutral commerce. As Ernest R. May has pointed out in a recent study of the neutrality period, by that time Grey had succeeded in establishing a moral basis for Anglo-American friendship capable of surviving new irritations and diplomatic controversies. In addition, German-American clashes over the submarine issue tended to relieve the pressure. Perhaps the early period of Anglo-American relations in the war could be most aptly described as one in which both sides manifested a will toward accommodation.

I

The protection of American commerce with Europe, both with neutral and belligerent countries, was one of the earliest concerns of the State Department. Under international rules and practices, a neutral was obligated to treat all belligerents in a spirit of equality and impartiality. In return, neutral citizens were permitted to trade freely with other neutrals in peaceful goods; trade with a belligerent could be intercepted by his enemy only if the commerce was of a military nature or when an effective blockade had been established which barred access to the opponent's ports and waters. It was hoped that the nation's interests could be promoted by belligerent adherence to the Declaration of London. Drafted at an international conference in 1909, the Declaration was a codification of maritime law which greatly circumscribed belligerent practices and favored the rights of neutrals. For those reasons it had not been ratified by the British government. The Declaration of London contained an extensive free list of goods, immune from capture even when shipped by a neutral to a belligerent port, sharply curtailed the number of absolute contraband materials subject to seizure upon interception, and defined a blockade of enemy coasts as legal only if effectively enforced. It was understandable, therefore, that the American government should request belligerent approval of the Declaration. The Central powers promptly complied but Great Britain, speaking for the Allies, gave only a qualified endorsement subject to several important modifications relating to the free list and indirect neutral trade with belligerents (broken voyages). Since such a compliance would not fully safeguard American trade and would leave room for unfavorable changes by other belligerents, the State Department renewed the request for an unqualified British acceptance.

Since both Wilson and Bryan apparently expected the war to be of short duration and were preoccupied with other affairs, the initial diplomatic exchanges were almost entirely in Lansing's charge. Exchanges with Grey revealed that the Allies were determined to block shipments of food to Germany through contiguous European neutrals. After the dispatch of a strongly worded request for an unqualified acceptance of the Declaration of London, Lansing at the suggestion of Colonel House entered into direct conversations with Ambassador Sir Cecil Spring-Rice. He first proposed that the British government assent to the Declaration and then negotiate agreements with European neutrals to restrict the reexportation of enumerated goods to Germany. When that failed to win approval, Lansing suggested that the Allies should approve the Declaration and follow the announcement by unilaterally proclaiming an increase in the list of contraband materials and asserting the right to restrict the commerce of noncooperative European neutrals.

The efforts failed. The British government was unwilling to restrict its freedom of action in the use of sea power. Grey assured President Wilson and other officials that Great Britain was trying to avoid unnecessary interferences with American commerce. He hoped that the American government would appreciate the exigencies the Allies faced in a war for survival and would therefore tolerate certain necessary maritime practices. Wilson clearly was moved by Grey's candid and friendly approach, and he wrote to Lansing that "The tone of it [Grey's letter] is so candid and sincere, and so earnest that I am sure you will wish to send our reply at once." [1] When the British authorities issued a new Order in Council announcing adherence to the Declaration of London with substantial modifications, the American government acquiesced and reserved its rights under existing international law. The British actions, after all, were defensible in view of American precedents established in the Civil War, and in any case most American trade was with the Allies. Although the negotiations by Wilson and Lansing have been severely criticized as a supine and disastrous diplomatic defeat, it would seem that they had done all that American duty and interests required.

II

Several neutrality policies were adopted in the fall of 1914 which in effect were favorable to the Entente cause. Some of the decisions appeared to be merely routine applications of practices long sanctioned by international usage. The unique characteristics of the European war, a bitter conflict in which the United States soon became the one great neutral, made these decisions of much greater significance than could have been reasonably predicted in 1914. Neutrality in the larger sense was more than a matter of legal definition and presumptive equality in policies relating to the belligerents. Genuine neutrality would seem to have required that the neutral must seek the substance as well as the appearance of impartiality and that it should not permit itself to become closely connected with either side. In practice

---

[1] Wilson to Lansing, October 15, 1914, *Foreign Relations, Lansing Papers,* I, 252.

the United States was soon almost inextricably involved in the Allied war effort, so that its neutrality seemed to some German leaders to be little more than a formality.

One of the apparently routine problems of neutrality related to the question of the defensive arming of belligerent merchantmen. It had been customary in previous centuries to arm such vessels for defense without the ships thereby acquiring the status of public ships of war. By 1914 it seemed to be an archaic practice of little significance in an age of fast, heavily armed naval vessels. When several British merchant ships equipped with guns arrived in American ports, the State Department issued a policy statement recognizing the right to defensive armaments and establishing criteria to distinguish defensive from offensive equipment. Although the German government promptly protested that such vessels were in fact armed for offensive purposes and therefore should be treated by neutrals as public warships, the American authorities brushed aside the objections. The incipient controversy disappeared when the British government, presumably to avoid costly delays in establishing the status of individual ships, decided to refrain from arming vessels coming to America. A year later the issue was renewed when several armed ships arrived in American waters. A dilemma resulted, for Germany plausibly asserted that such armaments were used offensively against the frail and vulnerable submarines when they surfaced for lawful challenges in accordance with the rules of cruiser warfare. No option remained, it was contended, but to utilize submerged attacks by U-boats without warning or safety provisions for those aboard the armed merchantmen. The American decision of 1914 thus operated unintentionally in favor of the Allies and complicated American policy toward the submarine issue.

The traditional American practice in regard to trade in contraband goods had been to permit private citizens to manufacture and sell, at their own risk, war materials to belligerents. As long as the traffic was legally open to both sides and the neutral government was not involved, international law sanctioned the commerce. Of course, in 1914 Allied needs and British sea power meant that the trade would be only with the Entente powers. This commerce began almost immediately after the outbreak of war and quickly reached such dimensions as to become essential to continued American prosperity. As the department's expert on international law, Lansing advised that the traffic was legal and fully compatible with the dictates of neutrality. He was also conscious of the impact of war purchases in stimulating the sluggish national economy. Finally, he believed that embargoes against the exportation of arms and war materials were unwise from the standpoint of general principles, as such prohibitions would in effect penalize peaceful states and reward planned aggression. Yet some voices, pacifist, pro-German, and neutralist, were raised in criticism of the trade as allegedly unneutral. Lansing therefore recommended issuance of a policy statement to clarify the status of the commerce. With presidential approval, the contraband trade circular of October 15, 1914, defended the legality and neutrality of the trade in arms and other contraband goods by private citizens. The statement thereby tacitly encouraged the continuation and growth of the commerce. Within a year, the flood of Allied orders was to bring new prosperity to America while greatly strengthening the Entente war effort. By 1915, an embargo which some critics earnestly sought would have had a severely depressing effect on the American economy. Despite the formal consistency of the trade with the rules of neutrality, its effects were to strengthen American bonds with the Allies and to create growing popular resentment and distrust in Germany.

An inconsistent course at first was adopted in regard to private credits and loans to the belligerents. Permission of the war trade would seem logically to have required acquiescence in its financing. Bryan, while apparently failing to appreciate the significance of the arms traffic, was convinced that a neutral should not permit belligerents to borrow money. As he wrote Wilson, "money is the worst of all contrabands because it commands everything else. . . ." [2] The financial interests created by loans would influence press and public opinion, he believed, and would make the preservation of neutrality more difficult. Furthermore, in permitting loans a neutral would in fact encourage the con-

---

[2] W. J. and M. B. Bryan, *The Memoirs of William Jennings Bryan* (Chicago: Winston, 1925), 375–376.

tinuance of hostilities by providing the financial sinews, while a prohibition would facilitate an early restoration of peace. President Wilson concurred, apparently influenced by the secretary's pacifist arguments and by a practical desire to safeguard the American financial structure from the immediate disturbances created by the war. A public statement was released on August 15, which asserted that "in the judgment of this Government loans by American bankers to any foreign nation which is at war are inconsistent with the true spirit of neutrality." [3]

The so-called Bryan loan ban was entirely compatible with the requirements of neutrality. Neutrality procedures traditionally permitted such decisions and only required a formal presumption of belligerent equality of status and treatment. In practice, of course, the ban operated to the disadvantage of the Allied powers, for they alone had full access to the American market and needed credit arrangements to facilitate a legal trade. Available Allied resources were soon depleted and it became apparent by the fall of 1914 that the prohibition interfered with the American interest in the growth of the war trade. Representatives of the Entente powers and American bankers began to call these facts to the attention of the administration and requested a change of official attitude.

In September the French ambassador spoke to Bryan of the need to permit the Allies to arrange short-term commercial credits with private American banking firms. The secretary apparently was sympathetic and agreed to study the problem. A few weeks later the Russian and French governments proposed the use of short-term treasury notes in payment of war purchases in the United States. It was argued that the notes were merely routine temporary credit arrangements to facilitate a legal commerce and that they were amply secured by Allied holdings and gold reserves. A spokesman for the National City Bank discussed the proposal with Lansing and, after pointing out that a public loan was not involved, he asserted that without the credit arrangement belligerent purchases in America would have to be drastically curtailed or halted. Lansing immediately

---

[3] *Papers Relating to the Foreign Relations of the United States, 1914, Supplement,* 580.

conferred with Wilson and it was agreed to inform the financiers orally that the administration would not object to the credit scheme.

Revisionist historians have tended to portray Bryan as the only genuinely neutral member of the Wilson administration and have emphasized that the relaxation of the ban was made during his absence from Washington and presumably without his approval. The evidence indicates that Bryan was informed and in fact did concur. He was inordinately proud of his authorship of the loan prohibition, which was praised highly in neutralist and pacifist circles, and understandably he apparently preferred to deemphasize the significance of the relaxation and his role therein. The credit decision was a large step toward complete reversal of the ban, for revolving credits actually amounted to a type of long-term loan. The decision, however, was not inconsistent with the formal dictates of neutrality and it was in accordance with the nation's economic interests.

Credit arrangements proved only a temporary expedient. By the summer of 1915 it was obvious that short-term credits would not suffice for the expanding war trade. Allied agents and representatives of interested American financiers again brought pressure on the State Department, this time for a complete revocation of the Bryan ban. The president of the First National Bank of Chicago, James B. Forgan, wrote that Great Britain had reached the point where it must either raise a large public loan in America or sell British-held American securities in large amounts (which probably would depress the stock market), and he requested a restatement of administration policy. Treasury Secretary William G. McAdoo also was alarmed at the situation and conferred repeatedly with the State Department.

McAdoo argued forcefully that the ban was inconsistent with the government's previous decision to acquiesce in the contraband trade. Lansing, who had replaced Bryan as secretary of state when the latter resigned in June 1915, was readily persuaded. He wrote Wilson that conditions required the complete revocation of the 1914 prohibition. American exports would exceed the value of two and a half billion dollars by the end of 1915, which the Allies could not pay without depleting gold reserves and precipitating a general bankruptcy. Lansing predicted that if large-scale loans were not raised in America, Allied purchases would necessarily cease and the inevitable result for the United States would be "restriction of outputs, industrial depression, idle capital, financial demoralization, and general unrest and suffering among the laboring classes." [4] Flotation of a large bond issue and banking loans would alone relieve the acute situation and ensure the continuation of prosperity in America. Furthermore, argued Lansing, the original reason for the prohibition no longer existed for the nation had a surplus of capital, while popular sympathy for the belligerents had already been formed and would not be affected by financial commitments. Lansing concluded the letter with a rhetorical plea: "Can we afford to let a declaration as to our conceptions of the 'true spirit of neutrality' made in the first days of the war stand in the way of our national interests which seem to be seriously threatened?" [5]

Although he declined to authorize a formal reversal, Wilson permitted oral assurances to the bankers and the issuance of a press report attributed to a "high official spokesman" to the effect that the administration did not object to the flotation of a belligerent loan. The way was thus cleared for the public sale of a large Allied bond issue. By April 1917 public issues and private banking loans to the Allied governments exceeded two billion dollars. Germany, in contrast, borrowed only twenty-seven million dollars. The bulk of the debt was adequately secured against an Allied collapse, however, by Allied and American securities and other collateral.

National self-interest clearly was the basis for the administration's reversal of policy. Continuation of the prosperity-inducing Allied purchases was the overriding consideration to the American policy makers. It has been contended that Wilson probably acted also to perfect American neutrality, because the ban allegedly was unneutral in hampering a legitimate trade. The president may have been so motivated, but if so he entered a most doubtful area of reasoning. International law did not

---

[4] Lansing to Wilson, September 6, 1915, *Foreign Relations, Lansing Papers,* I, 144–147.

[5] *Ibid.*

require a neutral to open its markets to belligerent purchases nor to facilitate the financing of such purchases. The 1914 ban had been completely compatible with neutral requirements, even if in practice it operated against America's interest in the war trade. The repeal deepened American economic entanglement with the Allies and perhaps increased popular sympathy as well. German leaders and the public were to become increasingly embittered by the one-sided trade with their enemy. Yet when full submarine warfare was launched in 1917, with the result of forcing America into the war, it was not in retaliation against the war trade but was a desperate effort at victory over the Allies. In any case, it would have been difficult for the American government to have declined to rescind the ban in 1915 for the economy would have been damaged, political unrest would have ensued, and the net effect would have been to harm the Allies to the benefit of distrusted Germany. Economic interests and sentiment, and possibly security considerations on the part of some Wilson advisers, rendered such a choice improbable.

III

By the spring of 1915 Sir Edward Grey was forced to assent to extensions of maritime warfare even at the price of strains in Anglo-American relations. Britain's allies were anxious for more vigorous economic measures against the enemy, and within England important elements, especially members of the Conservative Party, demanded drastic regulation of neutral commerce to completely cut off German imports. The result was a tightening of blockade techniques through nonexportation agreements forced on European neutrals, the use of controls over bunker supplies and cargo insurance in order to influence neutral trade, tighter censorship of mails, and the blacklisting of neutral firms allegedly trading with the Central powers. This system was in many ways less cumbersome and more effective than a formal blockade and to a large degree it fell within the scope of domestic rather than international law. It could be successfully challenged only by threats of neutral economic retaliation, which the American government never was willing to do on a serious scale. A combination of pro-Ally sentiment and economic ties, together with the goodwill and trust assiduously cultivated by Grey, sufficed to preclude a truly vigorous American reaction.

The Wilson administration responded to the Allied measures with lengthy formal protests and practical acquiescence. Lansing, along with Colonel House, played an important part in the process. Lansing was convinced that the interests of the United States required the avoidance of serious challenges to the Allied maritime system. He also was aware that in the Civil War the Union government had greatly extended belligerent practices and had set examples which Britain now utilized. In any case, he thought, war was an inhuman affair in which a belligerent fighting for survival could not be expected to show much consideration for neutrals. The best course, therefore, was to be patient and to file formal reservations of right pending a postwar settlement in the saner atmosphere of peace. He was not to take this tolerant attitude, however, when Germany resorted to ruthless underseas warfare. Wilson and House concurred in an acquiescent course and for the same general reasons. As Ernest May has commented, the administration could believe that in these decisions it was following the dictates of the national interest and yet complying with neutrality; to have done otherwise would have sacrificed vital economic interests and would have helped Germany.

The State Department cooperated informally with Allied control measures designed to prevent German imports through contiguous neutrals. Ambassador Page transmitted a proposal, in late 1914, that if the American government would not support diplomatically copper exports shipped by indirect routes to the Central powers, Britain would relax controls to permit American importation of rubber and other raw materials from the empire. Experts within the department helped to work out the arrangement and American firms began to cooperate with British blockade officials in exchange for advance clearances of exports to Europe. Several associations were established to facilitate cooperation, such as the Textile Alliance and the Rubber Association. Officially the State Department was not involved, but on an informal basis its agents arranged conferences between American exporters and British officials. British Ambassador

Spring-Rice confessed his bafflement at the contradictions between the official and unofficial attitudes of the State Department: "The attitude of the United States government is peculiar. They cannot recognize the Order in Council [blockade], but they are anxious to promote trade and therefore to assist as far as they can in the private negotiations. . . ." [6] The contradiction was more apparent than real, for Lansing with the wholehearted encouragement of House sought to submerge controversies in inconclusive and lengthy diplomatic exchanges. American commerce was promoted by the arrangements, one more example of the coinciding of American and Allied interests. The net result was to orient American neutrality even more benevolently toward the Allied war effort against Germany.

IV

Belligerent retaliations at sea in late 1914 and early 1915 seriously affected the United States. The first measure was the North Sea mining zone, proclaimed by Great Britain in November 1914 as an action necessitated by indiscriminate enemy use of mines. The entire North Sea was countermined and neutral vessels were advised to pick up sailing directions at Allied ports or to proceed at their own peril. Vessels stopping for instructions were naturally subjected to cargo inspection. Here seemingly was a close parallel to the subsequent German submarine zone, for if merchantmen had ignored the Allied warning and asserted the right to travel the high seas subject only to traditional belligerent challenges, eventually one or more would have struck a mine with probable loss of property and life. Both the Allied and German zones departed from previous international practice, though the U-boat was a greater and more shocking deviation, and both potentially endangered neutral rights, lives, and property. The American government, however, declined to join the Scandinavian neutrals in diplomatic protest and made

---

[6] Spring-Rice to Grey, April 23, 1915, in Stephen Gwynn, ed., *The Letters and Friendships of Sir Cecil Spring-Rice* (Boston: Houghton Mifflin, 1929, 2 vols.), II, 263–267.

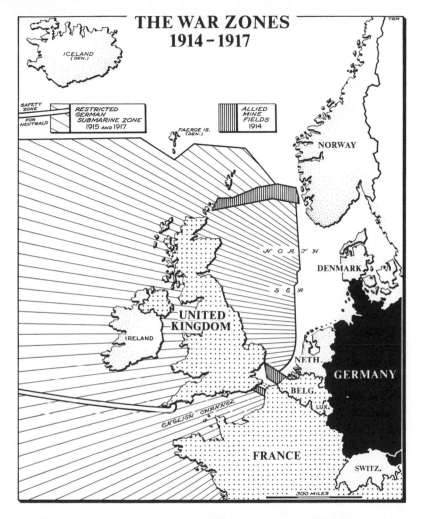

THE WAR ZONES
1914–1917

ICELAND
(DEN.)

SAFETY ZONE FOR NEUTRALS

RESTRICTED GERMAN SUBMARINE ZONE 1915 AND 1917

ALLIED MINE FIELDS 1914

FAEROE IS. (DEN.)

NORWAY

NORTH SEA

DENMARK

UNITED KINGDOM

IRELAND

NETH.

GERMANY

BELG.

LUX.

ENGLISH CHANNEL

FRANCE

SWITZ.

300 MILES

no formal objection to the mining zone. The failure to protest apparently reflected the fact that few American ships utilized the area and therefore no important interest was involved. International law was also unclear on the entire subject of mining. The decision to acquiesce indicated the differential character of American neutrality, for when the German government retaliated with the submarine zone, the United States was to demand the strictest compliance with its interpretation of international law.

Great Britain promptly exploited the German U-boat proclamation to complete the economic blockade of the Central powers. The Order in Council of March 11, 1915, announced that in retaliation all commerce with Germany would be interdicted, with compensation promised to neutrals for the resultant seizures. This was a "pseudo" blockade in the sense that an effective legal blockade under the generally established rules was impossible because of unimpeded German trade with neutrals in the protected Baltic Sea. In the absence of a legal blockade, international law provided that a neutral could freely trade with a belligerent in nonmilitary goods. This trade was now suppressed and the coasts and ports of European neutrals in effect were blockaded in order to prevent indirect importations by Germany. Although the German retaliation had been vigorously contested, the Allied measures were to bring comparatively milder American objections. The explanation again was that German actions threatened important American trading interests and lives as well, whereas that was less true of the Allied measures. The United States could adjust to Allied warfare without endangering its interests; it apparently could not do so with Germany.

Although some officials within the State Department desired a vigorous objection to the blockade on legal grounds and a full reservation of American rights, Wilson was inclined to acquiesce and thereby avoid a prolonged diplomatic debate. He was aware that maritime disputes between the two nations had led to war in 1812, and he was determined to prevent a similar embroilment. Lansing, though by no means wishing a sharp confrontation, did believe that the March 11 Order in Council required careful analysis and refutation lest the United States appear to accept the blockade as legal under international law. Wilson, on the other hand, thought that it was not worthwhile to debate points of legality and consistency with the British and instead preferred a reply which would express confidence that the Allies had no intention of blockading neutrals and would assume responsibility for any resultant violation of American rights. The president obviously was not then greatly disturbed at the British measures which he regarded as honorable even if departing from the strict letter of international law. Lansing persisted in the effort for a sweeping counternote and reservation of rights, and he pointed out to Bryan and Wilson that Britain in fact was preparing to blockade neutrals to interdict even noncontraband trade with Germany.

The president was only partly persuaded. The American note of March 30 did not directly question the legality of the blockade. The right of neutrals to trade with other neutrals in peaceful goods was asserted and the blockading of neutral coasts labeled a novel act. American rights were reiterated and the hope was stated that Britain would strive to avoid violation of the rights of neutrals. If not, the United States would expect Great Britain to make "full reparation for every act, which . . . constitutes a violation of neutral rights." [7]

The March 30 note has been described as indicating that Wilson tacitly accepted both the Allied and German maritime systems, with each belligerent warned that it would be held to a strict accountability for consequent violations of American rights. Yet the reply to the British blockade seems milder and more acquiescent. Germany was warned that it would be held to a strict accounting for American lives and ships lost by illegal submarine attacks; subsequent implementation of that warning revealed that the American response would include the severance of diplomatic relations. Great Britain, however, was not threatened with drastic countermeasures. Instead, assurance was expressed that Britain would avoid infringements of neutral rights or render full reparation. Chandler P. Anderson, a special counsel to the State Department, very aptly explained the note to the Republican leader, Elihu Root:

It is stern on the face of it but has a twinkle in the eye, and the important thing is that although it states our position strongly on international law, it contemplates a settlement of our differences on the basis of pecuniary compensation for damages.[8]

Nearly four months elapsed before the British reply was presented to the State Department. The crisis created by the *Lusitania* sinking had concentrated the attention of government

---

[7] *Foreign Relations, 1915, Supplement*, 152–156.

[8] March 29, 1915, Anderson Diary.

and public on the more dangerous issue. By July a degree of normality had returned as Washington and Berlin began informal negotiations for a settlement. It then became necessary to cope once more with the British trade interferences. Neither the president nor his advisers desired to hamper unduly or greatly embarrass the Allies in their war effort, yet serious issues were involved and public opinion demanded some action. As Lansing wrote Colonel House, "you know that my sentiments are almost, if not quite, identical with yours that the matter must not be carried too far or the demands made too peremptory." [9] Officials in the State Department, however, did have grounds for suspecting Britain of trying to expand its commerce with neutral Europe by restricting American exports to those areas under the excuse of belligerent necessity.

The British note of July 23 attempted to refute the American objections to the March blockade order and pled the special exigencies of the war as justification for controls on neutral commerce. Only in that way could a belligerent prevent its opponents from supplying their war needs through neighboring neutrals. American precedents in the Civil War were also cited, and Sir Edward Grey expressed his pleasure that the commerce of the United States was expanding as the result of Allied purchases which more than compensated for the loss of the German market. Though the experts in the State Department were less satisfied, President Wilson found the note a "strong case" in defense of British practices.

The problem of cotton illustrates the skillful and conciliatory approach of Grey and does much to explain why Anglo-American relations continued to be relatively calm. While America generally was prosperous, deprivation of the German market had caused distress in the cotton-producing southern states. Discontent was heightened by rumors, which events substantiated, that the Allies were preparing to retract an earlier promise and to declare cotton absolute contraband. Such a step would sharply curtail American raw cotton exports to the European neutrals contiguous to Germany. Grey found himself under tremendous pressure in England for the waging of more

_____

[9] Lansing to House, July 30, 1915, House Papers.

drastic economic warfare. A coalition cabinet had been recently formed, with a large "ginger" faction less interested in conciliating America. Elements in the Parliament and the public also made it impossible to delay energetic measures. Grey did not act, however, until the blow to the United States could be cushioned by a British arrangement to purchase at a specified price approximately the amount of cotton normally exported to the Central powers and thereby to prevent a slump in the cotton market. The American government, of course unofficially, found the arrangement to be satisfactory and, after brushing aside a German counteroffer as a palpable bribe to persuade the government to challenge the blockade, adjusted to the classification of cotton as absolute contraband.

On October 21, after still another delay occasioned by recurrent submarine crises, this time over the destruction of the *Arabic,* a long formal protest against the blockade was dispatched to London. Wilson was still inclined to trust Britain's good intentions, but as he wrote House, settlement of the *Arabic* controversy only made relations with Great Britain "more perplexing" for "apparently we have no choice now but to demand that she respect our rights a good deal better than she has been doing." [10] The note was a delayed triumph for Lansing. Earlier he had urged a full protest against the legality of the blockade but Wilson had declined in the belief that Great Britain would avoid unnecessary interferences with American trade. With at least a temporary lull in the U-boat issue, and with mounting pressure from shippers outraged at Allied detention of over three hundred neutral vessels, the president agreed that further action was mandatory. There was no intention, however, of crippling the Allied war effort and Colonel House assured the distraught Spring-Rice that the impending note would not wreck Anglo-American relations.

The protest aroused some excited talk of a crisis, particularly in England. Yet the note was without threat of any kind. As an editorial in the *New Republic* so aptly described it, the diplomatic missive was a legal protest of record which a benevolent American government did not intend to cause the Allies any

---

[10] Wilson to House, August 31, 1915, House Papers.

serious embarrassment. The protest described the blockade as illegal and ineffective and condemned Allied interferences with cargoes allegedly destined for the enemy through neutral ports, but it did not assert the right of neutrals to trade directly with Germany in noncontraband goods nor did it warn Britain that failure to comply with American demands would lead to drastic countermeasures. Instead, the note expressed the earnest hope that the Allies would be guided by legal principles, not expediency, and it was asserted that the United States would continue to defend neutral rights against lawless belligerent actions. The October note was in fact primarily a legal protest for the sake of the record and a postwar adjustment. Even as it was delivered, Colonel House was discussing with Sir Edward Grey a type of American mediation-intervention in the war in favor of the Allies. As Grey wrote the colonel, the American demands could not be met without abandonment of the blockade of Germany and he trusted that the United States would not "strike the weapon of sea power out of our hands and thereby ensure a German victory." [11] When the British government finally answered the protest, in April 1916, its reply was completely unsatisfactory. Lansing and the State Department then concluded that further discussion of the blockade issue was pointless.

V

The nadir in wartime Anglo-American relations came in the summer of 1916, after the *Sussex* pledge had permitted the submarine question to subside and in the midst of a feverish presidential election. In Great Britain, Grey was virtually powerless to resist the pressures for a further tightening of the blockade, and, as the controls over neutral commerce were extended, new irritants arose in relations with the United States. Public criticism in America of the blockade was increased by controversies over mail censorship and the open blacklisting of Ameri-

---

[11] Grey to House, November 11, 1915, in Charles Seymour, ed., *The Intimate Papers of Colonel House* (Boston: Houghton Mifflin, 1926-1928, 4 vols.), II, 79–80.

can firms. House and Lansing were greatly disturbed and feared that the outcry would compel the president and Congress to adopt strong retaliatory measures. Wilson was becoming increasingly displeased with the Allies both because of their trade interferences and because he was beginning to be persuaded that their war aims were nearly as selfish as those of the Central powers. Neither belligerent side, it seemed to him, was willing to support a truly reasonable peace settlement.

British efforts to control neutral mails became more stringent in 1916. To perfect the blockade and prevent enemy importation of contraband goods and intelligence information in letters and packages, neutral mail steamers were stopped on the open seas and forced into Allied ports for inspection. Many delays and seizures resulted and suspicions were aroused that Allied censors transmitted intercepted business information to competing English firms.

Lansing subsequently admitted that he conducted the mails controversy primarily as a matter of form and without vigor. A formal protest was mandatory, but he was convinced that the United States would soon probably be involved in the war and he did not want to restrict its future freedom of action. Several exchanges brought no substantial relief, for the British government justified its practices on the grounds of German abuses of the mails and the absence of a valid international agreement on sealed mails. Yet Lansing described the reply as friendly and helping to clear the atmosphere despite its failure to resolve the controversy. As he wrote Wilson a few days later, the United States possibly would not be neutral in a future war and should be careful not to commit itself too firmly to a principle which might subsequently be regretted. The president indicated approval of Lansing's tacit acceptance of the censorship measures.

While the presidential campaign was underway, Great Britain announced in July a blacklist which included eighty-five American firms and individuals. Suspected of trading with the enemy, these persons were denied use of all British-owned facilities. The blacklist did not seriously disturb the American economy, but it aroused great public anger especially since it followed other unresolved disputes over mails and the blockade. It seemed to indicate an almost complete disregard for American sensibilities and caused President Wilson to react sharply. He wrote House that it was the "last straw" and that he was contemplating a request to Congress for legislation to prohibit private loans and curtail exports to the Allies.

House and Lansing, the latter ill with diabetes, were apprehensive that drastic retaliation might ensue. Lansing left his sickbed to make a public address urging patience in dealing with the belligerents. He pointed out that there was a significant difference in the rights infringed upon by the belligerents, and in effect he stated that the property interests involved in Allied actions were less important than the loss of lives resulting from submarine attacks. His speech was so obviously pro-Ally that Ambassador Spring-Rice reported to Grey that Lansing had courageously attempted to stem the tide of public indignation. Colonel House recorded in his diary that he and Lansing had to cooperate to guide Wilson along the correct course and avoid a direct confrontation with the Allies.

The two advisers were not wholly successful for the president was determined to make the Allied governments appreciate the depth of American resentment at the blacklist. At his request, legislation was passed by Congress in September which authorized the executive to withhold clearances and port facilities from foreign ships which declined to transport American goods. The retaliatory legislation, however, fell far short of an embargo and it was never invoked. Commerce Secretary William C. Redfield provided the president and State Department with an analysis of Anglo-American trade which concluded that application of even so mild a retaliation would endanger the nation's prosperity. Closure of American ports to British ships would interrupt the war trade and probably lead to countermeasures. The country was too dependent on Allied purchases to jeopardize its economic welfare. The blacklist, and even the blockade, were minor irritants in comparison. Historian Ernest May doubts in any case if drastic measures would have forced Great Britain to retreat, for by 1916 the Allies had developed a large productive capacity in arms and munitions factories in England and Canada and were less vulnerable to pressure than they would have been earlier. Restrictions on the export of food and on loans, however, would have been more serious. Whatever the effects of possible American retaliation, it does seem clear that Great Britain would not easily have been persuaded to make significant concessions.

In addition to considerations of sentiment and economics, it seems probable that the political aspects also caused Wilson to stop short of drastic countermeasures. House and Lansing were both convinced that continued British friendship was of great importance and that nothing should be done which might align America on Germany's side or promote the triumph of the Central powers. Wilson was not unaware of such arguments and apparently shared them to a large degree. In January, prior to the most pronounced deterioration of relations, Ambassador Page had sent a well-reasoned dispatch to Washington which enunciated America's political interests in an Allied victory. The war should not be permitted to end in a stalemate, he wrote, since an indecisive result would ensure a renewed arms race and would disturb the Far Eastern balance of power where Japan sought large concessions as the price of cooperation. All depended on the American attitude:

If the United States should oppose the blockade [of Germany] and the war should end as a draw, Japan will be able to extort her full demands because England will need her Navy indefinitely on this side of the world. If the United States acquiesces in the blockade and the war ends with German defeat, both England and the United States will be in the way of Japan's aggressions. . . . The only hope therefore of a permanent peace lies in such a decisive defeat of Germany as will prevent a new era of armament and a new set of dangerous complications both in Europe and in the Pacific. . . .[12]

Lansing was in complete agreement. As his diary entries attest, his thoughts went further and included the conviction that American participation would probably be necessary to ensure Germany's defeat. Wilson was also impressed with Page's presentation and commented to Lansing that "the arguments it urges are evident enough and of considerable weight." [13]

---

[12] Page to Lansing, January 22, 1916, *Foreign Relations, Lansing Papers*, I, 306–307.
[13] Wilson to Lansing, January 24, 1916, *Foreign Relations, Lansing Papers*, I, 308.

CHAPTER IV

America and the U-Boat

IN CONTRAST TO ITS POLICY toward the Allied maritime system, the American government declined to make a similar adjustment to German submarine warfare. Few important interests were seriously affected by the British blockade, whereas many would have been jeopardized by a harsher reaction. Such was not the case with Germany. The ruthless use of the U-boat threatened America's economic ties with the Allies, enhanced the fear of some officials and citizens that Germany constituted a threat to the national security, and shocked the moral and humanitarian sensibilities of most Americans.

I

The German submarine campaign was begun early in 1915 almost accidentally and with little thought of the consequences. The High Seas Fleet, bottled up in the North Sea by the British Grand Fleet, had been frustratingly inactive in the war. When a few submarines achieved spectacular success in sinking several Allied ships in the fall of 1914, the navy leaders welcomed their use as a means to demonstrate dramatically the worth of their service. The German public responded enthusiastically to the promise of the new weapon and Chancellor Bethmann-Hollweg consented to its more intensive use. Ostensibly in retaliation to Allied mining of the North Sea, the Berlin government proclaimed on February 4, 1915, a war zone surrounding the British Isles. Within that area, Allied merchant as well as war ships would be subject to submerged U-boat attacks without warning and without the provision of safety arrangements for crews and passengers. Neutral vessels were warned to avoid these waters since alleged Allied misuse of neutral flags as a cover and the adoption of ramming techniques against surfaced U-boats precluded the normal practice of visit and search and thus rendered accidental attacks highly probable.

Since Bryan was absent from the department, Wilson and Lansing were primarily responsible for determining the American response to the German challenge. After conferences with the president, Lansing drafted a brief, sharp note which expressed grave concern at the submarine zone and condemned it as a violation of international law. Neutrals, it was asserted, had the right to travel on the high seas subject only to the normal belligerent practices of visit and search. Germany was solemnly warned that it would be held to a "strict accountability" for any destruction of American ships and lives which might result. After Bryan's return to the capital, the draft was further discussed before it was dispatched on the tenth of February. To the great delight of Bryan, always eager for a gesture of impartiality, the note was coupled with a simultaneous protest to Great Britain against use of neutral flags as a *ruse de guerre*.

Yet the two protests, however satisfying to Bryan and the public, were not equal in tone or portent. The note to Britain was without a threat of forceful measures in case of noncompliance, whereas the warning to Germany held that government to strict accountability for violation of international law affecting American ships and citizens. The February 10 note to Berlin expressed "grave concern," a very strong diplomatic phrase, and stated a readiness "to take any steps it might be necessary to take to safeguard American lives and property and to secure to American citizens the full enjoyment of their acknowledged rights on the high seas. . . ." [1] Although subsequent events revealed that Wilson had by no means decided on what measures would be taken if a warning did not suffice, clearly a very serious threat of retaliation was implied. The German chancellor so interpreted the note and, in the belief that an American entry into the war would be disastrous for the Central powers, he

---

[1] *Foreign Relations, 1915, Supplement*, 98–100.

began a two-year struggle against those Germans who advocated vigorous underseas warfare regardless of the costs.

The motives of Wilson and Lansing (House was then in Europe) apparently were to uphold the nation's honor and rights, and to defend its economic interests against the U-boat menace. Other choices were at least theoretically possible in early 1915: the American government could have acquiesced in the zone and requested all American ships and citizens to avoid the war area; or it could have insisted only on the safety of passenger vessels entering the prohibited zone; or a protest could have been made but settlements for any losses postponed until after the war. Some historians have pointed out that probably nothing less than complete avoidance of the zone and the consequent sacrifice of much of the war trade would have prevented an eventual clash, since ultimately the German authorities sought nothing less than a total blockade of the British Isles. Whether that was the only workable alternative, American policy makers in 1915 could not have been positive that there was no other choice. The fact is that President Wilson and most of his advisers rejected other policies as too costly to the national interest and honor.

II

The first of the submarine crises arose when an American citizen lost his life aboard the British liner *Falaba*, torpedoed in the Irish Sea on March 28. For the next four weeks American policy makers discussed with great thoroughness the implications of the sinking and the diplomatic alternatives available to the United States. Lansing advocated application of the strict accountability note to cover not only Americans aboard American ships but also nationals traveling on belligerent passenger vessels. In his view the sinking of the *Falaba* and the resultant drowning of the American citizen were indefensible acts contrary to international law and practice. A belligerent should abide by the rules of visit and search, and the destruction of a noncombatant vessel was never justifiable without adequate provision for the safety of those on board. Lansing recommended that a sharply worded note should be sent to the German government which would assert the rights of neutrals to travel the high seas subject only to normal belligerent challenges, denounce the destruction of the unresisting *Falaba* as a wanton and indefensible act, and request disavowal and reparations. Defense of the nation's rights, and an aroused public opinion, demanded such firm action even though it would amount to an indictment of submarine warfare in general. Secretary Bryan, on the other hand, was increasingly disturbed as the more dangerous aspects of the crisis were unfolded and he struggled for adoption of a course which would at least postpone a final settlement, if necessary, until after the war. Citizens who voluntarily entered the war zone, he believed, had contributed by their own negligence to their deaths and should not be permitted to involve the American government in unnecessary controversies. To do otherwise, he argued, would be to insist that the mere presence of an American aboard a belligerent merchant ship immunized it from submarine attack and would amount to an untenable condemnation of U-boat warfare. Bryan also advised that German resentment of the arms trade with the Allies should be considered in framing a policy, so that the United States would not seem to be partial toward the Allies and uncompromising in its relations with Germany. Although he sympathized with Bryan's passionate desire for peace, Wilson agreed with Lansing that the killing was illegal and that it was probably America's duty to protest the act and to insist that Germany abide by the requirements of international law. Although events were to overtake the administration before a final decision had been made in the *Falaba* case, the outline of the subsequent policy toward the submarine issue had begun to emerge.

The sinking of the *Lusitania* raised again in a more shocking way these basic issues of policy. The large British Cunard liner was torpedoed off the Irish coast on May 7, and sank in eighteen minutes with the loss of nearly 1200 lives including 128 Americans. Despite German press warnings about the dangers of traveling in the war zone, the killing of helpless noncombatants aroused a feeling of horror in America and led to a general condemnation of submarine warfare as immoral and uncivilized. President Wilson again faced several major questions: should the United States, as Bryan earnestly counseled, continue to display impartiality by coupling protests against one belligerent's actions with similar objections to the practices of the other? And how should strict accountability be defined? Bryan advised at the most a request for monetary damages and the expression of a willingness to postpone the final settlement until after the war. Lansing continued to state forcibly his convictions that law and rights required a firmer course. After an initial wavering, Wilson adopted that approach. Although he refused to be driven into war by emotional reactions to the sinking, he saw no alternative but a vigorous defense of American rights. Public opinion seemed to be clearly behind his course. Reaction in the eastern states tended to be more bellicose, but most Americans still hoped that war could be avoided without an abandonment of rights on the high seas. The president decided to separate the American case against Germany from controversies with the Allies, because he deemed it more serious and was persuaded that only in that way would the Berlin authorities be persuaded of the necessity to comply with his demands. Strict accountability was to be interpreted as immediate and full compliance with the American view of its rights, with a diplomatic rupture implied unless Germany yielded. His advice rejected, Bryan was to be forced to the point where he felt that his principles left him no choice but to resign from the State Department.

The principal arguments mustered by Bryan for a milder course were primarily extensions of the views he had earlier expressed in the *Falaba* case. Confirmation by New York customs officials that the *Lusitania* had carried some contraband materials, including cartridges, led the secretary to recommend that passenger vessels should not be allowed to transport contraband: "A ship carrying contraband should not rely upon passengers to protect her from attack — it would be like putting women and children in front of an army." [2] His emotional argument did not convince Wilson and Lansing, who believed that Germany did not have the right to destroy enemy merchant vessels without safety provisions regardless of the character

---

[2] Bryan to Wilson, May 9, 1915, *Foreign Relations, Lansing Papers*, I, 386.

of the cargo. Lansing countered other objections with strongly reasoned arguments that the strict accountability note had not discriminated between citizens traveling aboard American and belligerent passenger ships; to retreat now would indicate an earlier failure to warn travelers and would arouse a storm of criticism within the United States. Wilson agreed that Lansing's contentions were "unanswerable" and drafted a protest to Berlin which outlined the American view of neutral rights and expressed confidence that the German government would disavow such acts, offer reparations, and prevent future recurrences.

Bryan joined in the task of polishing the note "with a heavy heart." With some perspicacity, he feared that the United States was losing its position as an impartial friend of both sides: "Germany cannot but construe the strong statement of the case against her, coupled with silence as to the unjustifiable action of the Allies as evidence of partiality toward the latter. . . ." [3] Furthermore, growing pro-Ally sentiment in the United States would cause the note to be greeted as a prelude to war, and the probable Allied praise of the administration's stand would further embitter German opinion. These results could be avoided, he suggested, by bracketing the note with a protest to London against the blockade, and by releasing a press statement that strict accountability did not necessarily mean an immediate settlement for it might be advisable to postpone until after the war disputes which diplomacy could not presently resolve. Indicative of his own doubts about the next step and of a similar concern with the dangers of war, Wilson at first agreed to an informal press "tip" along the lines suggested by Bryan. Secretary of War Lindley Garrison and others, however, promptly objected and managed to dissuade Wilson on the grounds that the news "tip" would weaken the note and encourage Germany not to comply.

The disappointed Bryan then concentrated on an offsetting protest to the Allies. After the dispatch of the first American note on the *Lusitania* on May 13, Bryan had Lansing begin to draft a strong condemnation of the British maritime system. The reluctant counselor complied but he warned that to send

---

[3] Bryan to Wilson [undated], *Foreign Relations, Lansing Papers,* I, 392–394.

such a note at that time would arouse popular criticism by implying a parallel between German and Allied violations of rights and law. Wilson agreed and repeatedly declined to send a protest while the U-boat issue was unresolved lest it seriously weaken the American position and make a settlement less possible.

The German reply of May 28 was completely unsatisfactory. Bryan's unfortunate interview with Austrian Ambassador Dumba, eleven days earlier, apparently encouraged the German government to view the American protest as primarily intended for domestic consumption. Whether deliberately distorting Dumba's report of the conversation, a Berlin foreign office official informed Ambassador Gerard that Bryan had told Dumba that Wilson's *Lusitania* note was a concession to outraged American public opinion and was not to be taken too seriously. Bryan denied that version and secured a similar disavowal from Dumba. Probably his anxiety for a peaceful solution had caused him to be less cautious than was wise in conversation with the Austrian ambassador. In any case, the German reply charged that the *Lusitania* had been carrying troops and concealed armament, and was in fact a naval auxiliary; therefore, Germany was relieved of the obligation to observe the established rules of visit and search in dealing with the vessel. A final statement of policy, however, was reserved until these aspects of the sinking could be discussed further.

Secretary Bryan now found himself fighting a losing battle against adoption of a course which he believed would soon lead to war. Lansing analyzed the German reply as completely failing to acknowledge the principles involved: "The German note is not expressed in language which evinces a friendly sentiment for the United States. It shows an inflexible purpose to continue a course of action which this Government has frankly asserted to be illegal and inhuman."[4] A more vigorous attitude was required, he felt, and he recommended that the details of the sinking not be debated until the Berlin authorities admitted the validity of the principles involved. Bryan's fears and anxieties reached a peak as it became apparent

---

[4] Lansing to Bryan, June 1, 1915, *Foreign Relations, Lansing Papers*, I, 417.

that Wilson agreed with the counselor. At the cabinet meeting on June 1, when the president outlined a firm reply to Germany and was supported by Secretary Garrison and others, Bryan angrily exclaimed that some of his colleagues were guided by pro-Ally sentiment. The president sternly rebuked the disturbed secretary and again refused to weaken the American position by making a simultaneous protest against the British blockade. Wilson shared much of Bryan's concern but he was convinced that defense of the nation's rights and interests left him no feasible alternative.

Although Wilson urged him to remain in his post, Bryan could see no action consistent with his beliefs but resignation. His sympathetic wife has recorded that her husband returned from these crucial cabinet meetings exhausted in body and depressed in spirit. He often lay sleepless at nights, jotting down his thoughts as he sought desperately for a way out of the dilemma. It was now obvious to him that Wilson was determined to pursue a firm course even at the risk of a diplomatic rupture and possible hostilities. The president believed that America's rights and interests demanded nothing less, whereas to Bryan peace had to be preserved at all costs. In his view, nothing could justify war with Germany. As he exclaimed to his wife: "Why can't he [Wilson] see that by keeping open the way for mediation and arbitration, he has an opportunity to do the greatest work man can do!" [5]

All of Bryan's suggested alternatives were rejected. He urged arbitration or at least a prolonged investigation of the facts surrounding the *Lusitania,* in accordance with the formula of his beloved "cooling-off" treaties, prior to any decisive action. Again he recommended that citizens should be warned from traveling on belligerent vessels within the war zones and especially aboard ships carrying contraband. The Berlin government, he claimed, was seeking a face-saving device for meeting the American demands and it ought to be provided an opportunity for retreat. Undoubtedly, Bryan's suggestion that American ships and citizens be prohibited from the war zone if adopted would have removed most immediate possibilities of a clash

---

[5] Bryan, *Memoirs,* 420–421.

with Germany, for it then would have been the sole responsibility of the Allies to transport their purchases to Europe. Even the banning of Americans from traveling aboard belligerent vessels probably would have resolved the immediate crisis and perhaps would have made it possible for the United States later to have accepted completely unrestricted use of the submarine. These solutions, however, required the sacrifice of prestige, rights, and trade which President Wilson was unable to accept.

Bryan resigned on June 9, as the second American note on the *Lusitania* was forwarded to Berlin. Apart from his apprehension of war, Bryan apparently thought that his resignation would crystallize the latent desire of the American people for peace. He was disappointed, for though some groups and newspapers hailed his act as just and courageous, most newspaper editors took a hostile and critical view. He was charged especially with weakening the government's position at a critical stage of the negotiations with Germany. Criticism became more widespread when the second note was published and seemed to many readers to be no harsher than the first one signed by Bryan.

Though public opinion in general seems to have rallied behind the president's policy toward Germany rather than his own, Bryan had some insight into the nature and import of American neutrality. The policies adopted since the war began had rendered American neutrality benevolent toward the Allies and of lesser value to Germany. In contrast to the acquiescent attitude of the administration toward the British maritime system, Germany had been required to comply fully with the American view of international law and neutral rights. After the second *Lusitania* note, American prestige and national honor were committed to holding Germany fully and immediately accountable for U-boat warfare. German persistence in its course would clearly lead to a crisis culminating in the severance of diplomatic relations and probably in war. As Bryan foresaw, the decisions of Wilson had foreclosed other alternatives and rendered American policy comparatively inflexible. Yet to Wilson no other choice seemed possible. The dictates of national honor (a realistic as well as a moralistic concern, for effective diplomacy depends closely on national prestige or credibility), international law and morality, and the protection of vital foreign trade, all required a firm stand of opposition to the submarine war zone. Increasingly, national honor seemed to loom as the largest of these considerations. Ernest May has argued persuasively that although Wilson at a later period perhaps could have adjusted to ruthless warfare if only moral and economic considerations had been involved, he and his advisers were deterred by the clear loss of national prestige which would have resulted if the government seemed to retreat: "All believed that any appearance of concession or compromise would taint the reputation, the dignity, or the honor of the nation." [6]

III

The German reply of July 8 to the second American note still fell far short of satisfying Wilson's demands. It offered a pledge of safety for American passenger vessels traversing the submarine zone but denied that American citizens by their mere presence could be permitted to immunize enemy ships from attack. Germany was obviously unwilling to abandon or significantly restrict submarine warfare, yet the American government preferred to avoid a diplomatic rupture if at all possible. The third American protest, forwarded on July 21, rejected the German defense of the *Lusitania* sinking as "very disappointing" and warned that repetition of illegal acts affecting American lives would be viewed as "deliberately unfriendly." These exchanges were followed by a relatively quiet period of negotiations for an adjustment. In effect, Wilson had retreated from his earlier blanket condemnation of submarine warfare against enemy merchantmen, and accepted it as long as the customary rules were followed and American rights respected. Ambassador Bernstorff was warned by Lansing that war would result from further loss of American life as the result of ruthless U-boat attacks. Bernstorff correctly concluded that Washington did not wish to continue the diplomatic exchanges and was not adamant

---

[6] Ernest R. May, *The World War and American Isolation, 1914–1917* (Cambridge: Harvard University Press, 1959), 158.

for an immediate settlement of the *Lusitania* case as long as further incidents were avoided.

The brief period of quiet was ended by the torpedoing of the *Arabic*. A British White Star passenger liner, the *Arabic* was sunk on August 19 with heavy loss of life including two Americans. The issue precipitated by the *Lusitania* would now have to be resolved or German-American diplomatic relations undoubtedly would be broken. American prestige was too thoroughly committed for any other solution. As Lansing wrote the president early in the crisis, although most Americans did not want war, they did expect a strong policy by the government; otherwise, the position taken earlier on the submarine would seem a mere bluff and the United States would be humiliated.

Wilson's closest advisers were nearly unanimous in advocating a firm course. Colonel House recommended a diplomatic rupture even if it led to war. Lansing concurred and he tried to make such an eventuality more palatable to Wilson by pointing out that war with Germany would restore good Anglo-American relations and would assure the president a role at the peace conference: "it would appear that our usefulness in the restoration of peace would certainly not be lessened by a state of war between this country and Germany, and it might even be increased." [7] The president agreed with the analysis of his advisers and apparently shared to some degree their view that a victorious Germany would probably next turn its attention to the United States. Yet he rejected their advice for a more drastic course, primarily because of his love of peace and abhorrence of war. In addition, he felt a sense of duty to the nation and to the world at large which required caution and patience in dealing with a dangerous problem. He also was aware of the deep divisions among the people in regard to hostilities over the U-boat issue. Perhaps most important of all he still hoped to play the role of peacemaker in the war for the good of all mankind. Consequently, in both the *Arabic* and the *Sussex* crises, he

---

[7] Lansing to Wilson, August 24, 1915, *Foreign Relations, Lansing Papers*, I, 470–471.

adhered to a firm but milder course than advocated by his principal advisers.

In Germany, Chancellor Bethmann-Hollweg was caught in a dilemma. He had never been very optimistic about the utility of submarine warfare, though he was not opposed to its ruthless use on principle, and he was fearful that unless the U-boat issue was carefully handled, war with America would result. Such a conflict, he was convinced, would be fatal to Germany since the United States would bring almost unlimited finances, industrial and agricultural resources, and military manpower into the struggle. Yet he was under great pressure for all-out warfare from the submarine enthusiasts in the navy, the Reichstag, and the press. The kaiser, Wilhelm II, was more of a figurehead than an absolute ruler and was weak, vacillating, and increasingly dominated by the army high command. The chancellor himself was not a vigorous or daring leader but tended to be a temporizer and compromiser by nature. Fortunately he was temporarily aided by the military leaders who agreed that Germany's enemies should not be increased while the Balkan situation was threatening. They advised, therefore, a modification, not an abandonment, of drastic submarine warfare. For these reasons, Bethmann-Hollweg followed a course of making sufficient concessions to America to avoid war while not formally renouncing use of the underseas weapon. Any other course would probably have meant the chancellor's immediate fall from power, for the Conservative Party and press shrilly extolled the virtues of the U-boat and insisted that there was little to be feared from an American entry into the war.

Ambassador Bernstorff informed Lansing on September 1 that his government had accepted the United States demand of July 21 "in principle" and that "Liners will not be sunk . . . without warning and without safety of the noncombatants." [8] Although the pledge caused much rejoicing in the American press, the formal German note of September 7, which explained the sinking, was unacceptable to the president. Apparently Chancellor Bethmann-Hollweg believed that the pledge had sufficiently relieved tensions so that a gesture could be made to the German public. The German note charged that the *Arabic* had first tried to ram

---

[8] *Foreign Relations, 1915, Supplement,* 530–531.

the submarine, and consequently liability for its torpedoing could not be assumed. The crisis was therefore renewed, with the American government taking the position that the September pledge was worthless unless Germany acknowledged responsibility and liability for the *Arabic*. The chancellor quickly appreciated his mistake and a "settlement" was arranged in which the sinking was disavowed and reassurances given that instructions to submarine commanders precluded repetition. Meanwhile, to ease the crisis, German U-boat warfare was virtually suspended.

The closing of the *Arabic* case still left unanswered the larger question of the legality of ruthless submarine warfare. The *Arabic* pledge applied only to liners and not to all merchant vessels, and the question of defensive armaments on merchantmen allegedly justifying submerged attacks was unresolved. Only a truce had been achieved.

IV

The quandary of the Wilson administration was revealed by an ill-destined attempt to resolve the submarine problem. A large number of Americans apparently was opposed to a course which might culminate in war with Germany. Rumblings of discontent were audible in Congress and criticisms were hurled at the administration's allegedly pro-Ally policies. The position taken in the *Lusitania* and *Arabic* cases left the government little flexibility, yet signs indicated that another submarine campaign was impending. The *Persia*, an armed British ship, was sunk on December 30 and the event, portending apparently another crisis, led to sharp attacks on the administration's foreign policy and to the introduction in Congress of a resolution to prohibit Americans from traveling on belligerent vessels. Wilson concurred in a Lansing proposed *modus vivendi* as a means of solving the submarine problem by persuading the Allies to abandon the use of so-called defensive armaments on merchant ships in return for a German pledge to conduct submarine warfare in accordance with the rules of war. The American leaders also had been troubled by doubts about the fairness of demanding that a submarine make surface challenges and thereby risk destruction by defensively armed merchantmen.

The Allied governments, however, believed that a submerged submarine was less effective than a surfaced one, which could use its deck guns to shell ships, and they refused to abandon the right of defensive armament. The only result was to provide additional arguments for congressional critics of Wilson's policies when the abortive scheme was "leaked" to the press. The president had to exert the full powers of his leadership to defeat resolutions to ban armed merchantmen from American ports and to prohibit citizens from sailing on belligerent ships.

In Germany, Chancellor Bethmann-Hollweg was compelled by political and naval pressures to consent to unrestricted underseas warfare at least against armed ships. The resultant torpedoing on March 24, 1916, of the *Sussex*, an unarmed French channel steamer, indicated that the U-boat commanders either could not or would not distinguish between armed and unarmed vessels. Although no American lives were lost, the *Sussex* affair violated the *Arabic* pledge and reopened the U-boat controversy. The most serious of the crises was at hand.

Lansing and House were convinced that the time for mere diplomatic protests had expired. The secretary wrote the president, "We can no longer temporize . . . when Americans are being killed, wounded, or endangered by the illegal and inhuman conduct of the Germans." [9] Either diplomatic relations with Germany should be immediately broken or an ultimatum should be sent demanding disavowal of the act and discontinuance of ruthless underseas warfare. Colonel House, who came to the capital for conferences during the crisis, also supported Lansing's recommendation. Wilson, though affected by the counsel of his advisers, was most reluctant to risk war. His instincts for peace and his continued desires to mediate the war seemed to make him vacillating and incapable of reaching a decision. After receiving fuller details of the tragedy, Lansing drafted a strongly worded note to Berlin announcing a diplomatic rupture until the U-boat campaign should be discontinued. He and House then called on the worried president in the White House and insisted on a frank discussion of the crisis and of the draft

---

[9] Lansing to Wilson, March 27, 1916, *Foreign Relations, Lansing Papers,* I, 537–539.

protest. With the receipt of clear evidence of German responsibility for the attack and indications that the American public supported a vigorous stand, the president decided to adopt a firm course.

The American note of April 18 contained the explicit threat to break diplomatic relations unless Germany immediately declared an abandonment of submerged warfare against belligerent merchant and passenger vessels. In effect, it was an ultimatum without a specific time limit. Chancellor Bethmann-Hollweg's position in the crisis still was that hostilities with America would be a disaster and should be avoided even at the price of a complete suspension of submarine warfare. Bernstorff reported that compliance with Wilson's demands would be followed by energetic American measures against the British blockade and would probably facilitate belligerent negotiations for peace. Bethmann-Hollweg's opposition seemed doomed to failure, however, for the army high command joined the admirals in supporting full use of the submarine as the most promising means of achieving victory in view of the stalemate in the land war. In addition the one-sided American war trade with the Allies had created great bitterness in Germany and made most officials, including the chancellor, suspicious of Wilson's motives and policies. Fortunately the chief of the Admiralty Staff, Admiral Henning von Holtzendorff, suddenly changed his position. Although still professing faith in the promise of the submarine, Holtzendorff feared that an American entry would enable the Allies to continue the war despite an unrestricted U-boat assault, whereas if America remained at peace and forced Great Britain into permitting legal commerce with Germany, the Central powers would be able to preserve their favorable military situation and ultimately to win the war. The chancellor, therefore, was able to persuade the kaiser to capitulate to American demands. The *Sussex* pledge of May 4 promised that unresisting merchant ships would not be destroyed without warning and safety provisions. An ominous condition was attached, however, stating that if the United States failed to obtain Allied compliance with international law and freedom of the seas, Germany reserved its freedom of action.

The second major phase of the submarine controversy had

ended with a German pledge applying not only to passenger liners but to all belligerent merchantmen, armed or unarmed. A renewal of U-boat warfare, therefore, would presumably lead to an immediate diplomatic rupture. The *Sussex* crisis had so clearly committed American honor and prestige that virtually no room was left for further diplomatic maneuver.

CHAPTER V

Mediation and Belligerency

Preword. Wilson had long wanted to play an important role
in mediating the war. He believed that peace without a decisive victory for either side would be the best, if not the only,
foundation for a stable and just postwar world. As events made
it obvious that the United States might soon be forced into
the conflict, he also became anxious for early peace negotiations
as the only solution for the problems of neutrality. His mediation
hopes, shared largely by House but little if at all by Lansing,
thus reflected an appraisal that preservation of the existing
distribution of power was desirable. Even more decisive, however, was his idealistic desire to construct a postwar world
freed from future wars.

I

As 1915 ended with indications that a new submarine campaign was in the offing, the president sent Colonel House overseas on his second peace mission. The first one, in early 1915,
had renewed his acquaintance with the belligerent leaders and
had provided some insight into their war goals and their determination to fight until decisive results had been obtained. House
had returned to America in June, during the *Lusitania* crisis,
convinced that the prospects for successful mediation were
exceedingly remote and that the United States would probably
soon be forced into belligerency. In the fall of 1915, additional
submarine incidents increased this conviction and he began to
nurture a scheme for mediation-intervention. Correspondence

with Sir Edward Grey indicated that Britain might be interested in a compromise peace if America would join a postwar collective security system. A plan was therefore to be developed whereby at a time deemed favorable by the Allies, Wilson would propose a conference of the belligerents; if Germany declined to attend or after entering the conference rejected reasonable peace terms, the United States would probably enter the war on the Allied side. Apparently House believed that America would soon be forced into war by the submarine if peace were not promptly restored, and he saw the plan as offering Wilson a satisfactory way to try to mediate the war and, if that failed, to enter it on sounder and broader grounds than the submarine issue. His desire for peaceful mediation was genuine, though he viewed a partial Allied victory within the framework of the current balance of power as most desirable from the viewpoint of American interests. The president was less convinced that a war entry was inevitable, though he realized that the situation was ominous and might well culminate in a diplomatic rupture with Berlin. He seems to have viewed House's scheme primarily as a means to terminate the conflict by diplomatic intervention before America could be engulfed and less as a possible way to enter the hostilities.

In October House told Wilson that if Germany triumphed, the United States would then bear the brunt of its enmity: "Therefore, we should do something decisive now — something that would either end the war in a way to abolish militarism or that would bring us in with the Allies to help them do it." [1] On the same day, House also stated to Lansing's principal subordinate in the State Department, Counselor Frank L. Polk, that Germany could not be permitted to defeat the Allies and become "the dominant military factor in the world. We would certainly be the next object of their attack." [2] Subsequently the colonel disclosed his plan to Lansing. As he argued to the secretary, the Wilson administration was obliged by duty to do what was wisest even if it met with popular disapproval, and that "it was clear it would not do to permit the Allies to

---

[1] October 8, 1915, House Diary.
[2] House Diary.

go down in defeat, for if they did, we would follow in natural sequence." [3] Although Lansing had some doubts about the handling of detailed questions of boundaries and colonies which would arise at the projected conference, he concurred with House's view of the need to prevent a victory by the Central powers. He promised to favor a strong course and, as House later urged, to cut German-American relations to a single thread.

House arrived in Europe in January 1916 and in conferences with Grey completed the understanding. Known as the House-Grey Memorandum, it provided for a conference to be called by the United States at a time deemed opportune by the Allies; if the Berlin government declined, the United States would probably enter the war against Germany; if the conference met but failed to achieve peace, the United States would leave the conference as a belligerent on the Allied side. Earlier in Paris, House also agreed with the French leaders that the United States would not invoke the scheme if the Allies scored military successes in the coming months, but that if the reverse were true, Wilson would act. The United States, he asserted, would not permit France to be defeated.

The colonel ignored many indications that the Allies, particularly France, were actually opposed to a negotiated peace as long as there was any hope of victory. As Arthur Link points out, House thereby deluded himself and Wilson into the belief that Britain and France were ready for mediation, when in fact Grey had apparently not taken his "agreement" with House very seriously and had entered into it largely to humor the desires of the influential colonel. House returned to the United States in March 1916, bearing the memorandum and filled with enthusiasm over his great success. The delighted Wilson then approved the plan but added still another qualifying "probably" to the statement that if Germany rejected a reasonable peace, America would enter the fray.

On this and the previous visit, Grey had managed to impress House, and therefore Wilson, with the moderation and reasonableness of Allied war aims; Germany's chancellor, Bethmann-Hollweg, was less successful for the precarious party truce in

---

[3] October 13, 1915, House Diary.

Germany and the existence of ardent annexationists made it very difficult for the chancellor to encourage Wilsonian mediation or to outline peace terms. Germany therefore seemed to the American leaders as more selfish and extremist in war aims, although actually the Allied secret treaties for postwar allocation of the spoils were of a similar nature.

Subsequent efforts during the *Sussex* crisis and after to invoke the memorandum and mediate the war aroused little response in London and Paris. The Allies apparently viewed American involvement as inevitable and as a consequence felt little need to bargain for it. In any event, they were unwilling to enter negotiations while Germany held the military advantage. Wilson eventually became convinced that the Allies were nearly as selfish in war aims and were as determined on full victory as Germany. Furthermore, the deterioration of Anglo-American relations in mid-1916 as the result of controversies over the blacklist and mail censorship, together with indications of a widespread desire for continued peace among the American people — revealed by the presidential election campaign of that year — strengthened Wilson's neutrality.

Avowed interventionists were few in America prior to the events of early 1917. Individuals such as Theodore Roosevelt, George Harvey of the *North American Review,* Lawrence Abbott of *The Outlook,* and others spoke and wrote on the probable need for intervention against Germany, and in 1915 the American Rights Committee was established to propagandize on similar themes, all apparently with only limited public effect. More influential were advocates of greater national efforts for military and naval defense against unnamed potential foes (though Germany was clearly implied). The National Security League worked tirelessly for military preparedness and its publications emphasized America's relative impotence. At first resistible, these pressures together with the even more persuasive crises abroad — the submarine issue and the Allied blockade — forced Wilson to endorse the cause of preparedness, which he ably defended in a series of addresses in early 1916 as necessary to protect the Western Hemisphere and defend the nation's honor, rights, and commerce on the high seas. Although he succeeded in getting most of his program through Congress, it was only after a sharp struggle with pacifist groups and with many Progressives, who viewed preparedness as a major step toward militarism and war and a defeat to the cause of domestic reform. In the 1916 presidential campaign, Wilson had to appeal to these elements in order to defeat the once more united Republican Party and he did so by portraying the Democrats as the party of neutrality and progressive reforms. The slogan "He kept us out of war" was one of the Democrats' most powerful appeals, whereas the Republican nominee, Charles Evans Hughes, was successfully portrayed as one who might lead the nation into war against Germany and Mexico. Wilson won a very narrow victory over Hughes and obviously owed it to an important degree to the widespread sentiment for peace.

The majority of the American people thus seemed to expect Wilson to preserve American peace even at the price of a partial retreat on neutral rights. Yet by the fall of 1916 reports from Europe indicated that a renewal of submarine warfare was virtually inevitable. The president realized that he could no longer delay a major peace move, even if it was distasteful to the Allies. His mediation efforts in the winter of 1916-1917 were thus desperate attempts to end the war by a negotiated peace before America was forced in by the U-boat.

Lansing opposed mediation as foredoomed and unwise, and House agreed that it could only embarrass the Allies. Upon being informed of Wilson's plans, the secretary recorded in his diary the fear that such a move would be resented by the Allies, because the existing war map would favor German gains in any peace negotiations: "on no account must we range ourselves even indirectly on the side of Germany." [4] Efforts in behalf of mediation would certainly fail, whereas if Wilson would only face facts he would realize that the "true policy" was to join the Allies in crushing imperialistic and autocratic Germany. Lansing was also critical of Wilson's plans for a postwar collective security organization to eliminate war and ensure a stable and just postwar world. The projected league of nations was objectionable to the secretary as a supranational authority

---

[4] "The President's Attitude toward Great Britain and Its Dangers," September 1916, Private Memoranda, Lansing Papers.

and because of the many practical problems it would create of defining boundaries and invoking collective action to prevent or subdue aggression.

II

With the distractions of the election over, Wilson began to act on his mediation plans. House and Lansing were convinced that the Allies would reject any offer. When the president informed him in November that a peace move was necessary, House objected that it would embarrass the Allies and might result in a more reasonable response from Germany than from its opponents. Wilson had planned to send House to Europe as part of the peace move, but the colonel demurred and Lansing joined him in a successful effort to eliminate that part of the plan. Wilson then submitted for their criticism a draft proposal for mediation which would demand that the belligerents state their war goals. Both House and Lansing objected to what they regarded as unfortunate wording of the proposal and managed to soften the note by changing the demand for war goals to a request. The warning that future American policies depended upon a frank enunciation of belligerent aims was also deleted. Even so, Lansing apparently was not satisfied with the note as finally sent but only viewed it as less objectionable than the original draft. More disturbing were indications that Wilson was prepared to retreat on the submarine issue. When the British merchantman *Marina* was torpedoed without warning and House branded it a violation of the *Sussex* pledge, the president replied incorrectly that the German promise had only applied to passenger ships. He then stated that he did not believe the American people wanted him to enter the war against Germany regardless of how many citizens might be lost through underseas warfare. The two advisers disagreed and believed that a sufficient cause already existed for breaking diplomatic relations. Lansing expressed their fears about the mediation offer when he indicated to Wilson the dilemma it posed: "But suppose that the unacceptable answer comes from the belligerents whom we can least afford to see defeated on account of our national interest and on account of the future principles of liberty and democracy in the world — then what?"[5]

What indeed? The fact was that although Lansing and House were persuaded that the national interest and ideological considerations required a German defeat and that American involvement was almost inevitable, Wilson was emotionally more than ever committed to keeping America at peace. He concurred in part with his advisers' analyses but he was now less sure than before that the cause of the Allies was America's cause. Preferable would be a general peace settlement with the United States assuming its proper role in the establishment of a postwar society of nations. Even the arrival of a German peace bid, therefore, did not alter his plans. On December 12 the German government requested the United States to transmit to the Allies a proposal for the beginning of direct peace negotiations. In the belief that an American peace move would seem to be part of the German overture and would not be given serious consideration by the Allies, Lansing and several others urged Wilson to delay his own effort. The president declined and the request for a statement of belligerent war aims was dispatched on December 18. As expected by many, reaction in the Allied countries was adverse. Resentment was expressed at Wilson's apparent bracketing of the war aims of the Allied and Central powers as on the same moral level. Ambassador Page reported that British officials were deeply hurt and angry, and the king had "wept." Germany wanted direct negotiations with its opponents, not Wilsonian mediation, therefore its reply was disappointing and failed to mention terms. The Allied response was more conciliatory and listed certain war goals, but a covering letter from the British foreign secretary made it clear that the Allies believed they could achieve their ends only through victory over Germany. Thus neither side was willing to state openly, or at least fully, its war aims and both belligerent camps were in fact opposed to permitting Wilson a large role in the eventual peace settlement.

In a final effort at forcing negotiations, Wilson decided to

---

[5] Lansing to Wilson, December 10, 1916, in *War Memoirs of Robert Lansing* (New York: Bobbs-Merrill, 1935), 179–180.

address the Senate, outlining the type of settlement which could be capped by a league of nations and appealing to the belligerent governments and people to end the costly slaughter. When Lansing was shown the draft of the speech, he especially tried to persuade Wilson to delete the phrase calling for "peace without victory," which he argued was certain to arouse Allied hostility, particularly since an English spokesman had recently stressed the need for a decisive triumph in the war. He failed to change the speech in any significant way and it was delivered to the Senate on January 22, 1917, as a call for peace discussions and the framing of a settlement based on justice. Again, no positive results were achieved. Except for liberal elements, most of the Allied press reacted with hostility to the call for a peace without victory. Passions were so embittered that neither side could admit that a mere restoration of the status quo would be acceptable. Morale within the belligerent countries would have collapsed completely, with unpredictable consequences for the governments involved. The Allied response to Wilson's request for a statement of war aims clearly revealed their determination to secure large reparations and to destroy German military power. A statement of war goals finally obtained from Germany was equally unsatisfactory, indicating annexationist demands at the expense of France, Belgium, and Russia.

III

The failure of Wilson's peace efforts and the Allied rejection of the German overture presaged the end of American neutrality. The German government decided on an immediate campaign of unrestricted submarine warfare as the best hope for victory and accepted the virtually inevitable result of American belligerency.

Within Germany a shift in power was underway which made it almost impossible for the leaders of the civilian government long to delay a decision for a renewal of the underseas war. Field Marshal von Hindenburg and General Erich Ludendorff had succeeded to the control of the army high command and Kaiser Wilhelm deferred to these two popular military heroes. In the navy, Admiral Holtzendorff, who had supported the chancellor during the *Sussex* crisis, was persuaded by the submarine faction to endorse plans for an all-out U-boat war. Politically, the chancellor had sought to uphold public morale in the face of the mounting sacrifices demanded by the war and to continue the precarious truce among the several parties in the Reichstag. Since the parties were in disagreement about the goals of the war — with the Conservatives demanding extensive territorial gains and the Center Party for moderate expansion, while the Social Democrats advocated a peace without annexation and greater democratization of government at home — Bethmann-Hollweg dared not discuss openly Germany's war goals or reply positively to Wilson's overtures. Yet he, with others in the government, was convinced that unrestricted submarine warfare would mean an absolutely disastrous war with the United States. He sought to postpone that decision — his position was apparently too weak to oppose it outright — in the hope that either peace negotiations could be contrived while the war map favored Germany or that Wilson could be sufficiently impressed with Germany's reasonableness that unrestricted U-boat warfare would not lead to American belligerency.

Bethmann-Hollweg failed in both efforts. The chancellor hoped to hasten Wilson's peace moves, with the American president to serve as an initiator but not as a participant in any resultant negotiations, and to make a direct German initiative in the aftermath of recent victories in the Balkans. If these efforts proved unsuccessful, he planned to announce a restricted submarine offensive against armed ships only, in the expectation that such a measure would not drive the United States into the conflict and would prove as effective as a total campaign. The German overture was made on December 12 and was rejected by the Allies. In the interval, Wilson made his appeal for a statement of war aims. An unfortunate Lansing press statement, to the effect that the president's note to the belligerents indicated how near the United States was to involvement in the hostilities, helped cause the kaiser and his military leaders to view Wilson's request as offered in collaboration with Great Britain and as designed to force a conference with neutral participation. Therefore, the chancellor in effect declined to make a positive reply to Wilson. He too tended to share the suspicion of Wilson's motives resulting from the general benevolence of American neutrality toward the Allies. In thus failing to grasp Wilson's overture, Bethmann-Hollweg ruined whatever opportunity there was for creating a situation in which the United States would accept without war a new submarine campaign.

Failure of the peace campaign was followed by the final decision for unrestricted underseas war. At a conference at Pless on January 9, Bethmann-Hollweg repeated previous arguments against unrestricted warfare as inescapably leading to conflict with America. The military leaders were unpersuaded and concluded that the United States had already done Germany as much damage as it could through the war trade. They were confident that an all-out U-boat campaign against shipping around the British Isles would crush the enemy and bring victory long before America could raise and transport troops to France. Despite his skepticism about the success of the underseas campaign, Bethmann-Hollweg realized that further resistance was futile and he capitulated. Although he could have subjected the claims for a submarine campaign to a more detailed analysis and refutation, he had struggled long and persistently against the fateful decision.

The German announcement of the immediate launching of unrestricted submarine warfare was handed to Secretary Lansing on January 31. All ships, neutral or belligerent, would be destroyed without warning within the war zone around the British Isles. The announcement had been preceded by indications that the Berlin government was at least going to proclaim a campaign against armed enemy merchantmen. In discussions of that problem, Wilson informed Lansing that he had grave doubts about the legality of armed merchantmen and he indicated an apparent willingness to accept drastic U-boat tactics against such vessels. Even after the January 31 announcement revealed that Germany had gone beyond that point and was repudiating the *Sussex* pledge, the president was most reluctant to face the issue. House and Lansing joined efforts to persuade him that the national honor permitted no other cause but a prompt severance of diplomatic relations with Berlin. The two advisers also urged the need to check German militarism and serve the cause of universal democracy and future peace. Wilson seemed to them to be unaffected by ideological arguments. He retorted on one occasion that American involvement might endanger the future of "white civilization" in the world, apparently by disturbing the existing balance of power and leaving Japan free to expand in the Far East. He also indicated his belief that America could best serve the world by remaining a neutral and disinterested power helping to establish a just peace. Lansing tried to refute such arguments by asserting that a declaration of war would give the United States a prominent place at the peace conference. Most members of the cabinet agreed with the views of Lansing and House.

Wilson finally capitulated to the counsel of his advisers and to the logic of the situation. Past policy assertions of strict accountability left no alternative except a humiliating retreat. Yet the president still wanted to avoid actual hostilities and hoped that Germany might yet restrain the U-boat campaign. When he announced to Congress, on February 3, that diplomatic relations had been severed with Germany, he stated that he found it difficult to believe that Germany would really repudiate its pledges; only "actual overt acts" would convince him, but if "American ships and American lives should in fact be sacrificed . . . I shall . . . ask that authority be given me to use any means that may be necessary for the protection of our seamen and our people." [6]

The period from February 3 to April 2 was one of transition from peace to war. In the interval, submarine outrages and publication of the British-intercepted Zimmermann telegram — German Foreign Secretary Arthur Zimmermann proposed to the Mexican government that in the event of war with America an alliance should be concluded between the two states (and possibly with Japan as well) against the United States, with Mexico to recover territory previously lost to its grasping neighbor — prepared the American people psychologically for the struggle ahead. The Zimmermann telegram especially aroused popular

---

[6] *Foreign Relations, 1917, Supplement 1,* 109–112.

anger and convinced the country that Germany's intentions were hostile and aggressive. The period also was one of a tortured transition for President Wilson. With a disturbed feeling that continued American neutrality might be the only assurance for a stable postwar world, and torn between his concepts of national honor and concern for humanity on the one hand and on the other filled with a deep abhorrence of war, he appeared for a time to be incapable of making a clear decision. Although he had been compelled to break diplomatic relations with Germany, only with the greatest reluctance could he bring himself to contemplate war. At the time when the submarine announcement had been made, and after the failure of his mediation overtures, he apparently had decided on a diplomatic retreat. He foresaw that continuation of the bloody struggle would further weaken neutral rights and was prepared to retreat from the previous American position to accept U-boat assaults on armed merchantmen and perhaps even against all enemy vessels except passenger liners. After the German declaration, he apparently considered several courses for the United States short of full-scale hostilities: armed neutrality, in which American merchantmen would be defensively armed against the marauding submarine; or a limited naval war through use of naval forces to convoy shipping and destroy attacking U-boats. Gradually he came to dismiss these alternatives as too costly and unsatisfactory, as they had all the disadvantages of war without its compensations of purposeful and decisive effort and of an assured role at the general peace negotiations.

Wilson's advisers almost despaired at the delay and apparent vacillation. House, Lansing, and a majority of the cabinet members, with ill-concealed impatience, were convinced that full entry into the war was desirable and inevitable. But several presidential efforts to avoid hostilities still had to be endured. First came Wilson's appeal to other neutrals to follow America's example in breaking with Germany, in the hope that this would persuade Berlin to halt unrestricted submarine warfare. After that effort failed to attract any great support among neutrals, Wilson tried to detach Austria-Hungary from Germany and thereby to set the stage for an immediate termination of the war. Though war-weary and desperately anxious about a threatened dismemberment if defeated by the Allies, the Austrian government was too dependent on Germany to act separately.

Meanwhile the nation drifted ever closer to belligerency. After receiving a copy of the Zimmermann telegram, the angry Wilson requested congressional approval to arm American vessels in defense against lawless U-boat attacks. Despite a filibuster in the Senate by a small number of determined noninterventionists, led by Robert M. La Follette of Wisconsin, which prevented legislation, he subsequently discovered existing statutory authority and ordered American merchant ships to carry naval gun crews. In mid-March the sinking of three American vessels, the *City of Memphis*, *Illinois*, and *Vigilencia*, revealed that "overt acts" had taken place and that Germany was carrying out its threat to destroy all shipping, enemy and neutral, within the war zone. Lansing argued to Wilson that these deed certified Germany's hostile intentions and he suggested that the recent Russian Revolution, which replaced the autocratic czarist regime with a provisional republican government, made the time psychologically opportune for a declaration of war. House also joined in emphasizing the need for the final step. The weary and troubled president at last accepted the inevitable and on April 2 requested Congress to recognize that a state of war existed with Germany. After asserting that the issue with Germany left no alternative but hostilities, the president turned to the more lofty goals for which the nation would fight and called for a war to make the world "safe for democracy." Although there was no widespread enthusiasm for war, most citizens seemed to concur that the nation had been forced into belligerency in order to defend its rights against the challenge of the German submarine.

A survey of sixty-eight newspapers has revealed that only one opposed intervention after war was declared, whereas the others stressed submarine warfare as compelling the nation to resist in self-defense. Also stressed in the editorials was some fear of an attack upon the Western Hemisphere if Germany triumphed in Europe. These sentiments were reflected in the speeches in Congress, which generally concentrated on the U-boat issue and ignored Wilson's references to a league of nations as a goal of the war. Opponents to intervention argued that war was unnecessary and charged that the nation was being propelled into belligerency by profit-seeking industrialists and financiers. The vote on the war resolution thus revealed substantial opposition, with six voting against in the Senate and fifty (to 373) in the House of Representatives. A state of war was formally declared on April 6, 1917.

IV

American involvement in World War I, as in most other wars, defies simplistic explanations. In the 1930's the historical debate was polarized into the "submarine school," best represented by Charles Seymour, and the "revisionists," with Charles C. Tansill as the most effective spokesman. Seymour dismissed political and economic factors as at most peripheral causes of the war entry and instead emphasized the submarine challenge to American rights and lives. Tansill overlooked security aspects of the war and emphasized American unneutrality, the economic and sentimental ties to the Allies, as pulling the United States into conflict. Neither approach suffices to explain so complex an event. Seymour probably was right in the contention that there would have been no war without the submarine issue, for otherwise Germany and America would not have had a direct clash of interests and power. But the U-boat challenge alone does not explain why the United States adopted the strict accountability policy, since other alternatives were at least theoretically possible. As for the revisionist charges of unneutrality, it seems clear that American neutrality in fact was benevolent toward the Allies and grudgingly technical toward Germany. This did not result from deliberate planning, however, but rather from previous emotional and cultural affinities and from wartime economic connections with the Allies. In any case, Germany did not launch unrestricted submarine warfare merely from anger at the United States or just to cut off the arms trade. Although a different American posture perhaps could have influenced German policy along a more moderate course, the final decision for full underseas warfare was undertaken as the best remaining hope for decisive victory over the Allies through starving Britain into submission.

Just as clearly the hypothesis that the United States went to war in 1917 primarily to protect an endangered security against an immediate threat is not satisfactory. Although Lansing and House, and occasionally Wilson, thought of Germany as a menace to American security and stability, it was primarily as a future danger rather than an imminent peril. Yet Wilson was indeed far more practical in his policies and thinking than many scholars formerly believed, and he sought to promote the national interests as he envisioned them. Aided by his advisers, who exerted considerable influence on him, Wilson adopted policies that embodied economic and prestige interests, as well as moral considerations. The tacit acquiescence in the war trade and the permission of credits and loans to the belligerents reflected primarily economic interests; whereas the strict accountability policy toward U-boat warfare combined economic and moralistic factors with a desire to uphold the nation's prestige and honor as essential to any worthwhile diplomatic endeavors in the future including mediation of the war. Thus policies toward the Allies were favorable or benevolent because America's basic interests were essentially compatible with British control of the seas and Allied utilization of the American market. The course adopted toward Germany, on the other hand, was firmly nonacquiescent. Submarine warfare endangered American economic connections with Europe and as well violated moral sensibilities and affronted the national honor.

Among high administration officials, Lansing appears to have held the clearest conviction that American security would be endangered by a German triumph and that intervention in the struggle might be necessary — by late 1916 he believed it *was* necessary — to prevent that possibility. Although he sometimes indicated complete concurrence with Lansing's views, Colonel House believed that the most desirable culmination of the war would be enough of an Allied victory to check German ambitions but with Germany left sufficiently strong to play its proper role in the balance of power and to check Russian expansionism. A desire to preserve the balance of power, in the sense of ending the war short of victory for either side, was a factor behind the mediation plans of House and Wilson in 1915 and 1916.

Why did the reluctant president finally decide that belligerency was the only possible answer to unrestricted U-boat warfare? Why did he not rest content with the diplomatic rupture, or with armed neutrality or a limited naval war? The answer seems to have been that the prestige and honor of the nation were so committed as the result of previous policies that nothing less than a diplomatic break and a forceful defense of American interests were possible. By 1917 the evidence suggests that Wilson feared that a German victory was probable and that it would disturb the world balance, and although he was not apprehensive about an immediate threat to the United States, he did believe that such a result would endanger his idealistic hopes for a just peace and the founding of a new and stable world order. He referred to Germany as a madman who must be restrained. He finally accepted the necessity for actively entering the war, it would appear, with the submarine as the precipitant, only because he believed that larger reasons of national prestige, economic interests, and future security so demanded, and above all because of his commitment to the cause of an enduring world peace.

CHAPTER VI

The Moral Leader of the World

T HE TERM IDEALIST has been overworked in reference to President Wilson. Though idealistic in thought and phrase, his entire career from academic administrator to chief executive officer of the United States revealed a considerable capacity for common-sense appraisals and adjustments. One does not often secure or long hold high political office unless one possesses a large measure of practicality. In foreign policy, since the United States in general was a satisfied power which sought no additional territory and benefited from peace and stability, clashes between ideals and practical interests tended to be minimized. Wilson could advocate the lofty goals of a peace without vindictiveness and a global collective security organization because such ends were not only admirable in themselves but served an enlightened national interest. President Wilson also was generally practical in the pursuit of his goals. Viewed from the standpoint of the tasks he faced in guiding the nation from neutrality and isolation to belligerency, it is difficult to criticize Wilson's war diplomacy. He unified his people in a great war effort, helped disarm the enemy psychologically through his statements of war aims, and won the concurrence of rather reluctant allies to his program for peace. His chief mistake, it would seem, was to have taken too lofty a note to the American people when perhaps more frequent references to their economic and political stake in a stable postwar order might have avoided much of the subsequent disillusionment and reaction after the passions and idealistic fervor of the war had subsided.

I

President Wilson apparently at first had thought that American participation in the war would be confined primarily to economic and financial contributions, with the navy to help cope with the U-boat menace. As Allied needs became more fully known, however, it became apparent that victory would necessitate the training and transportation to the western front of vast numbers of American troops. The United States as a consequence was soon feverishly converted to a wartime economy. Miracles of production were achieved and nearly four million troops raised and trained. By the end of the war, General John Jacob Pershing commanded over two million American troops in western Europe. The American government also lent billions of dollars to the Allies to finance their purchases of war materials and foodstuffs in the United States.

A series of special Allied missions came to the United States soon after Congress declared war in April 1917. President Wilson was hesitant about receiving them and was apprehensive that the American people might conclude that the Allies were trying to influence and control the nation's war effort. The practical need to utilize Allied experience in civilian mobilization and to coordinate the production and procurement of supplies, however, caused the president to welcome the missions. His initial doubts were nevertheless significant as an indication of an underlying but persistent distrust and suspicion of the aims of the Allied governments.

The British mission, led by Foreign Secretary Arthur J. Balfour, arrived in the early spring of 1917, as did the French, and these were followed by Italian, Belgian, and other groups. Received with pomp and ceremony, the missions created great popular interest and helped to dramatize the collective nature of the war effort against imperial Germany. Balfour addressed a joint session of Congress, while President Wilson listened in the galleries, and in his speeches and appearances contributed to a diminution of Anglophobia in the United States. Practical gains also were achieved in improved liaison and the beginnings of coordinated procurement of war supplies. Later in the fall of 1917 Wilson sent Colonel House to Europe with an American technical mission to promote greater cooperation in the areas of finance, munitions, shipping, blockade, and military activity. A Supreme War Council to concert strategy was then established at Paris, but when the Allied governments insisted that it should also undertake political coordination, Wilson refused and limited American participation to nonpolitical functions. His motive, it seems clear, was to retain diplomatic freedom to formulate American war goals and to prevent the Allies dictating the terms of the eventual peace settlement.

The president also revealed mistrust of Allied purposes and the resolve to pursue an independent diplomatic course in his insistence on referring to the coalition as the "Allied and Associated Powers," with the United States obviously in the latter category. In this way a distinction was implied between the war aims of the United States, only recently in the war, and its cobelligerents in Europe and the Far East. No doubt the rather clumsy nomenclature also in part reflected the traditional aversion to military alliances, but the important factor seems to have been Wilson's suspicion of Allied aims and his determination to achieve a reasonable peace settlement.

Wilson and Secretary Lansing, despite subsequent denials to the Senate Foreign Relations Committee, were aware prior to the peace conference of the existence of the secret treaties among the Allies which provided for territorial gains after the war. These treaties and agreements, such as the 1915 Treaty of London between the principal Allies and Italy, were not necessarily evil but were in fact the inevitable results of a coalition war. To Wilson, however, they represented old-fashioned imperialism which would endanger the future stability and peace of the world. During his visit to America, Balfour had revealed most of the terms of the territorial arrangements whereby Germany's colonies were to be apportioned among the victors and important territories in Europe and the Near East would be similarly allocated. Discussions of these treaties with Balfour, apparently at House's advice, were kept entirely on an unofficial level. The only major agreement of which the American officials were not then informed apparently was that relating to

Japan's acquisition of the German holdings in Shantung Province, China. Subsequently, information was received by the State Department about Shantung as well as those arrangements relating to Europe. There can be little doubt that the president and his secretary of state knew the essential details long before the peace conference convened. The official attitude, however, remained one of indifference and formal ignorance:

This Government is not now and has not been in the past concerned in any way with secret arrangements or treaties among European powers in regard to war settlements. As to the secret treaties [released in Russia] . . . the Department has no knowledge of their existence or their terms except through reports emanating from the Bolshevik press.[1]

Aware of these arrangements to divide the spoils, Wilson wrote House that "England and France *have not the same views with regard to peace that we have* by any means."[2] Yet to discuss postwar settlement at that time would only precipitate disagreements and a probable weakening of the war effort, to the benefit of Germany. He hoped, therefore, by dissociating the United States from the Allies, to postpone the question of peace terms until the enemy had surrendered. Then he expected to utilize America's great financial power and influence to nullify the secret territorial arrangements and to achieve a just peace. Although the distinction between the United States and the Allies was in some ways an unfortunate one, since it did nothing "to break down the hoary isolationist ideal"[3] in America or to prepare the people for an internationalist course after the war, it was defensible as a means to avoid any implication of commitment to the Allied goals or a disruptive discussion of peace terms during the war.

---

[1] F. L. Polk to Representative J. T. Helfin, March 13, 1918, State Department File 861.00/1398, National Archives.

[2] Wilson to House, July 21, 1917, Baker, *Wilson, Life and Letters*, VII, 180–181. Italics are Wilson's.

[3] Thomas A. Bailey, *Woodrow Wilson and the Lost Peace* (New York: Macmillan, 1944), 20–22.

II

Peace societies had flourished in America and western Europe for over a century, and had begun to develop schemes intended to preclude international war. "Liberals" here and abroad were deeply convinced that warfare was a blot on civilization, an atavistic element in human society which could and should be eradicated. Besides the world was too economically interdependent and modern weapons unbelievably destructive to permit a recurrence of warfare. Many peace advocates saw the solution in the supplanting of alliances and balances of power by an international concert of power which would achieve stability and promote disarmament. As a means to this end, the secret diplomacy of the past must be discarded and the current war ended by a peace treaty whose enlightened terms would create the basis for new world order. Boundaries should be drawn in accordance with nationality principles, colonial peoples should not be callously bartered, and the exaction of indemnities and heavy retributions by the victors should be eschewed. In the United States an organization called the League to Enforce Peace was established in the spring of 1915 to work for a collective security system to eliminate war and promote world stability. The league advocated codification of international law, adjudication of disputes not yielding to diplomatic solutions, and the use of collective economic and military reprisals against aggressor states. Headed by former President William H. Taft, the organization carried on effective propaganda for its cause. A similar movement, known as the League of Nations Society, existed in Great Britain.

Wilson adopted the liberal peace program as his own and in moving and lofty phrases made himself the foremost spokesman of hopes for a just peace and a promising future. Increasingly the president's thinking concentrated on a collective security organization, an enlarged Monroe Doctrine which would embrace most of the nations of the world, as the capstone for a lasting and equitable peace. Since youth he had dreamed of a "parliament of man" which would usher in a golden era of progress. As president, he had supported a proposed Pan American Pact in 1914-1915 which would have established a type of miniature league in the Western Hemisphere. One of its provisions called for mutual territorial guarantees, which foreshadowed the collective security structure and especially Article X of the League Covenant. Although the pact failed of adoption, owing to Latin American rivalries and suspicions, it was to provide inspiration for Wilson's league concepts. In addition, House's correspondence with Sir Edward Grey in 1915 and 1916 also suggested the possibility of the United States helping to underwrite the peace through participation in some kind of collective security system. Grey seems to have envisaged a reconstitution and enlargement of the early nineteenth-century concert of European powers to preserve the peace.

By May 27, 1916, Wilson had sufficiently crystallized his thoughts to deliver a memorable address to the League to Enforce Peace. He publicly professed his faith in a concert of power to eradicate war and to ensure a reign of international law and justice. Wilson stated to the audience that although the causes and objects of the European war were not of concern to America, its destructive effects on neutral rights and trade were. Of necessity, therefore, the United States was deeply concerned with the peace which should end the struggle: "We are participants, whether we would or not, in the life of the world. . . . What affects mankind is inevitably our affair as well. . . ." It was America's desire to promote a peace containing future guarantees, "an universal association of the nations to . . . prevent any war begun either contrary to treaty covenants or without warning and full submission of the causes to the opinion of the world — a virtual guarantee of territorial integrity and political independence." [4] Subsequently he reiterated America's interests in freedom of the seas, disarmament, and protection against aggression through collective security in his appeal to the belligerents for a statement of war aims on December 18, 1916, and his address to the Senate on January 22, 1917. Even when Germany's declaration of unrestricted submarine warfare forced Wilson to take the nation into the con-

---

[4] *Congressional Record*, 64th Congress, 1st Session, Vol. 53, 1069–1070.

flict, his message to Congress still called for a just peace without conquests, to make the world "safe for democracy."

After American entry into the war, President Wilson utilized a series of notable addresses to seize the initiative as the formulator of liberal goals for the Allied and Associated states. In a Flag Day address on June 14, 1917, he drew a distinction between the German people, with whom America assertedly had no quarrel, and their military masters who had forced war on the United States: "we are not the enemies of the German people and . . . they are not our enemies," for "The war was begun by the military masters of Germany." If Germany's leaders succeeded in their imperialistic ambitions, "America will fall within the menace. We and all the rest of the world must remain armed . . . and must make ready for the next step in their aggression. . . ." [5] A peace merely restoring the status quo without fundamental changes would be premature and should be avoided, he warned, while the United States and its associates gathered strength in a peoples' crusade for freedom and justice for all.

In distinguishing between the German people and their rulers and in calling for the continuation of the struggle until full victory had been achieved, Wilson was trying to achieve two nearly irreconcilable goals. He believed that the war must be waged until Germany's militaristic leaders and their traditions had been thoroughly vanquished, for otherwise the sacrifices of war would have been wasted and the causes of future conflicts left to wreck the peace. This required girding American opinion for a bitter and protracted struggle. On the other hand, he did not want the war to produce such a blind hatred of all Germans as to preclude a reasonable settlement once the fighting was over. He also hoped to use this distinction to weaken German morale and hasten the termination of the war. In the latter case, some success was realized, but it is doubtful if many Americans were in fact able to restrict their war hatreds, which reached a level of hysteria on occasion, to the kaiser and the other German war leaders.

In August 1917 Pope Benedict XV invoked Christian prin-

---

[5] *Congressional Record*, 65th Congress, 1st Session, Vol. 55, 332–334.

ciples and addressed an appeal for peace negotiations to the belligerents. Apparently reflecting mounting peace sentiment, especially in certain German circles and in Austria-Hungary, the papal note proposed a settlement without reparations and indemnities, and based on disarmament, freedom of the seas, and restoration of occupied territories and captured colonies. All other questions should be left to further negotiations for adjustment. The Allied governments reacted negatively, fearful that it was a clever German device, made possible by close ties existing between Vienna and the Vatican, to escape just punishment. They viewed the suggested terms, therefore, as completely inadequate, and it was intimated that a concerted reply should be made to the pope. Wilson was embarrassed because the papal appeal generally reiterated views and principles similar to his own. His advisers also were in disagreement about the proper response. Secretary of State Lansing viewed Benedict as acting, probably unwittingly, as a German agent for he believed that a settlement on that basis would clearly favor the Central powers: "It is carrying the Christian doctrine of forgiveness a long way. . . . To make peace by accepting guaranties from the military rulers of Germany would only be to postpone the struggle [,] not to end it." [6] He advised a rejection of the proposal. House, on the other hand, believed that he had more accurate sources of information on European opinion and he advised a reply designed to appeal to liberal and pacifist sentiment on the continent and yet to leave the door ajar for possible negotiations based on a restoration of the prewar status quo. At first not inclined to make a formal reply, Wilson finally sent a vigorous note to the Vatican that concurred in the desire for peace but rejected mere restoration of the status quo as an inadequate foundation for a stable and just postwar world. Lansing in a sense thus scored over House, for Wilson's reply was in essence a ringing call for victory and the removal from power of Germany's military rulers. Once more Wilson had drawn a distinction between the German people and their alleg-

---

[6] Lansing to Wilson, August 20, 1917, *Foreign Relations, Lansing Papers*, II, 44–45.

edly evil leaders. The Allies were reassured, their fears that Germany would escape defeat by a diplomatic maneuver exploiting the supposedly naive Wilson silenced at least for the time.

The establishment of the Inquiry in the fall of 1917 was evidence of Wilson's increasing concern with war aims and preparations for the peace conference. It also revealed that Wilson was far more practical than usually assumed in seeking extensive information about belligerent war aims and exploring how American principles might be applied to the details of a settlement. As a recent study has concluded, Wilson's idealism "was tempered by a realistic awareness of the serious obstructions" [7] which his program for peace would face. House had been gathering materials for some time and Lansing was contemplating similar activities within the State Department. The president, however, regarded Lansing with misgivings and seriously considered requesting his resignation in 1917. He felt that the secretary was out of harmony with his policies and was so lacking in real ability as to be a serious handicap. House, with a higher regard for Lansing's abilities and anxious to avoid his replacement with a new secretary perhaps less amenable to his special role in foreign affairs, managed to dissuade the president. Lansing was continued in office but clearly he lacked Wilson's confidence, and his role thereafter was in many ways less significant than it had been in the neutrality period, with the nadir to come at the peace conference. It was understandable that the president should turn to House to organize a group of scholars to begin studies in preparation for the peace settlement. Perhaps also he viewed the task as not properly a diplomatic one. In any case he requested House on September 2, 1917, to create an organization under his supervision for those purposes. Although no doubt disappointed, Lansing graciously concurred and gave the project as much support as he could. As House recorded in his diary, "Lansing's attitude is just what I expected. I have never found the slightest trace of petty jealousy

---

[7] Lawrence E. Gelfand, *The Inquiry: American Preparations for Peace, 1917–1919* (New Haven: Yale University Press, 1963), 313.

in him so far as I am concerned." [8]

The Inquiry which took shape under House's general direction consisted of a group of scholars, primarily in history and the social sciences, totaling about 150 members. With headquarters at the American Geographical Society building in New York City, the group was directed by Dr. Sidney E. Mezes, House's brother-in-law and president of the City College of New York. Isaiah Bowman of the geographical society subsequently became Mezes' executive officer and other notable men such as David Hunter Miller, James T. Shotwell, and Walter Lippmann were associated with the group. Despite problems of organization and a shortage of real experts and research materials for a study of certain areas, the Inquiry performed much valuable work. Divisions were created to study geographical areas ranging from Europe to Latin America and the Far East. In fact, because of the special interest of Bowman and the State Department in Latin America, a disproportionate amount of time and effort was concentrated on an area remote from the probable work of the peace conference. Nearly 2000 reports were compiled on geographical, economic, and political problems that might arise at the peace negotiations and hundreds of excellent maps were acquired or prepared. The papers differed greatly in quality and usefulness, ranging from factual to analytical studies and with some reports very inadequately researched by special pleaders for one or another of the nationality groups seeking gains at the peace settlement. Although the Inquiry completed its work and ceased to exist after January 1919, a number of its members accompanied Wilson to Paris and served as experts and delegates on the various commissions established by the conference. Its work, in the form of factual material and specific recommendations, was of considerable value and made a definite impression on the resultant peace treaties. Without it, Wilson would have experienced even greater difficulties in achieving his goals. The work of the Inquiry also largely dispels the charge that one of the causes of Wilson's failures at the peace conference was lack of preparation for the peacemaking.

---

[8] September 20, 1917, House Diary.

III

President Wilson generally had avoided formulation of more specific peace goals until the fall of 1917. The wartime coalition otherwise would have been strained unless America acquiesced in the "selfish" purposes of the Allies. Apparently he also viewed himself alone among the war leaders as sufficiently impartial to speak for the true interests of mankind. Events in the fall and winter, however, persuaded him to seek a joint statement of principles and goals with the Allied statesmen. The Socialist Congress meeting in Stockholm, Sweden, revealed the growing desire for a quick peace and opposition to an imperialist war in European labor and radical circles. The Bolshevik seizure of power in Russia in early November, followed by an armistice and by appeals for immediate peace negotiations on the basis of no annexations and no war indemnities, seemed to necessitate a counterstatement of Allied war aims to refute charges of crass imperialism. No doubt Wilson also hoped to strengthen the cause of a liberal peace. The need to reassure liberals of the justice of the Allied goals became all the more imperative when the Bolshevik authorities began to publish the Allied secret treaties for a division of spoils upon the conclusion of the war.

When House was sent to Europe to confer with the British and French governments on military cooperation, he was instructed by Wilson to request agreement to a joint pronouncement on war aims which would answer Bolshevik and socialist charges and would serve as a clarion call to the world for the eradication of militarism and the triumph of righteousness. House brought the proposal to the attention of the inter-Allied conference meeting in Paris, but he met with little encouragement. The British prime minister, David Lloyd George, objected that it was unnecessary to repeat previous statements on the purposes of the war. Furthermore, he held that it would be most inopportune to do so in the wake of the recent Italian military disaster at Caporetto and the defection of Russia from the war, for Germany would interpret it as a sign of Allied weakness.

French Premier Georges Clemenceau agreed. The colonel reported that even a very general statement to the effect that the Allied and Associated powers were fighting not for gain but to eliminate militarism and promote a peaceful world order met with no enthusiasm at Paris. Probably the cold reception of Wilson's suggestion not only reflected Allied preoccupation with military and morale problems but even more an unwillingness to permit the American president to brush aside the secret treaties and to impose his own concept of a desirable peace.

After the return of House, Wilson decided to act unilaterally. He requested the Inquiry to prepare a memorandum for a public statement of war aims. The State Department was in effect ignored in the entire affair, with Lansing only belatedly called in for consultation. The colonel encouraged Wilson, convinced that the contemplated address would arouse enthusiasm and support in liberal circles in Great Britain and on the continent. The resultant Inquiry memorandum, largely the work of Mezes, Miller, and Lippmann, was presented by House to the president on January 4, 1918. Wilson and House then reworked the material into a typical Wilsonian document that was more generalized than the Inquiry memorandum to avoid possible difficulties with the Allies and in keeping with the president's penchant for exhortation and sweeping pronouncements. In addition, the Inquiry recommendations had placed greater emphasis on strategic and economic factors, whereas Wilson was to accentuate the concept of the self-determination of peoples based on nationality principles.

The Caxton Hall address by Lloyd George on January 5 almost dissuaded Wilson from delivering his remarks. Lloyd George's speech, which was moderate in tone and referred to the need for an international collective security organization, anticipated many of Wilson's main points. House persuaded the hesitant president, however, to deliver his address as planned. Reiteration of liberal goals was desirable, he argued, and this was an excellent opportunity to demonstrate the essential harmony of Anglo-American war purposes.

At noon on January 8, President Wilson appeared before a joint session of Congress to deliver the memorable Fourteen Points Address. After referring to the Bolshevik negotiations for peace with the Germans at Brest-Litovsk, the president enunciated fourteen points as the "program of the world's peace":

1. "Open covenants of peace, openly arrived at," with diplomacy to proceed frankly and openly thereafter and secret arrangements or treaties not to be countenanced;

2. freedom of the seas in peace and in war, with the high seas not to be closed except to enforce international agreements;

3. the removal insofar as practical of barriers to the equitable flow of trade and access to markets;

4. reduction of armaments to the lowest level consistent with national security;

5. an adjustment of colonial claims based on the interests of the colonial peoples involved as well as the interests of the claimant power;

6. evacuation of Russian territory and cooperation to permit Russia "the independent determination of her own political development and national policy. . . ," for the treatment given Russia by other states would constitute "the acid test of their good will";

7. evacuation and restoration of Belgium;

8. all French territory "should be freed" and invaded portions restored, with the wrong done France in 1871 in regard to Alsace-Lorraine to be righted;

9. "A readjustment of the frontiers of Italy . . . along clearly recognizable lines of nationality";

10. autonomy for the peoples of the Austro-Hungarian empire;

11. evacuation and restoration of Roumania, Montenegro, and Serbia, with Serbia to be assured access to the sea;

12. autonomous development for the peoples of the Turkish empire;

13. an independent Poland comprising territories inhabited by indisputably Polish people and with secure access to the sea;

14. "A general association of nations must be formed under specific covenants for the purpose of affording mutual guarantees of political independence and territorial integrity to great and small states alike." [9]

---

[9] *Congressional Record*, 65th Congress, 2d Session, Vol. 56, 680–681.

The response to President Wilson's speech was generally most favorable at home and abroad. It has been described as "democracy's answer in its first full-dress debate with international communism." [10] It of course was more than a ringing retort to Bolshevik charges that this was merely an imperialistic war between rival camps of capitalistic states. Wilson sought to mobilize the consciences of well-intentioned men everywhere and to express what he regarded as the universal longing for a peace that would rectify ancient wrongs and usher in a new age of peace and justice. More specifically he gave notice to the Allied governments that American goals were diametrically opposed to the secret treaties and the schemes of vengeance against Germany. The address aroused great praise in the United States, even from such outspoken opponents as Theodore Roosevelt. Beneath the surface, however, some Republicans and nationalists were critical of phrases that seemed to imply a possible weakening of tariff protection against foreign imports, and not all were enthusiastic about the responsibilities which the concept of an association of nations foreshadowed.

In Great Britain and on the continent, liberal circles were inspired by the address and increasingly viewed Wilson as their spokesman. Clemenceau of France, however, simply ignored the speech, though he had congratulated Lloyd George on his efforts of January 5. The leaders of the British government were privately skeptical about the meaning of Wilson's reference to freedom of the seas. In other particulars there had been no great difference between Lloyd George's Caxton Hall speech and Wilson's address; perhaps, as one historian has noted, if it had not been for Wilson's tendency to distrust Great Britain, the two states could have collaborated to mutual advantage on an agreed joint program of war goals. Finally, although the Bolsheviks and the German leaders reacted adversely to the speech, thus limiting the immediate impact, the long-range effects of this and similar speeches was to encourage German liberals and socialists to distrust the policies of the imperial German government. George Creel's Committee on Public Information even-

---

[10] A. S. Link, *Wilson the Diplomatist: A Look at His Major Foreign Policies* (Baltimore: Johns Hopkins University Press, 1957), 104.

tually flooded Germany, Russia, other areas in Europe, the Far East, and Latin America with sixty million pamphlets and leaflets embodying Wilson's Fourteen Points and other pronouncements. Such overselling on the idealistic goals of the war undoubtedly prepared the way for later disillusionment, but as a war measure helping to arouse the American and Allied peoples and to some degree to weaken the morale and stamina of the Central powers it was a bold psychological weapon.

In subsequent addresses Wilson added other points or enlarged on previously enunciated goals as the basis for a liberal peace. A total of twenty-seven particulars, some repetitive, eventually were pronounced. On February 11 the president again addressed Congress. After describing the reactions of the German chancellor to the Fourteen Points address as almost completely inadequate, he called for peace based on four general principles. Each part of the peace settlement must reflect the demands of justice for that particular problem and must help promote an adjustment that would facilitate a permanent peace; peoples and provinces were not to be exchanged and bartered as mere pawns in the game of balance of power; each territorial adjustment must be made in the interests of the people directly involved; and the nationalistic aspirations of peoples should be met to the greatest degree possible without creating or perpetuating antagonisms and discords dangerous to the peace of Europe and the world. Again, liberal circles in Europe were delighted with their champion, while German and Austrian spokesmen admitted the acceptability of the principles but expressed doubt that the Allies would consent to negotiate on such an enlightened basis. When the Central powers imposed a harsh treaty with vast territorial losses on Bolshevik Russia at Brest-Litovsk on March 3, Wilson in early April utilized a war bond drive address to flail Germany for its imperialism: "We are ready, whenever the final reckoning is made, to be just to the German people, [to] deal fairly with the German power, as with all others." Yet the actions of the German leaders in imposing a drastic peace treaty on prostrate Russia revealed what imperial Germany would do elsewhere if its arms triumphed. The only possible response by the United States and its associates was to use "Force, Force to the utmost, Force without stint or limit, the righteous and triumphant Force which shall make Right the law of the world, and cast every selfish dominion down in the dust." [11] Wilson was more than ever persuaded that a just peace required the complete defeat of the Central powers.

In a speech at Mount Vernon on July 4, the president emphasized the need for peace built on an international organization representing the rule of law derived from the consent of the world's peoples and supported by the force of world opinion. On September 27, at the opening of the Fourth War Loan drive in New York, Wilson stated additional principles or points which the peace should achieve and he particularly emphasized a league of nations as indispensable to the realization of impartial justice. The league's constitution should be a definite part of the postwar settlement, and upon this new organization would devolve the responsibility for guaranteeing the peace.

The immediate impact of these later addresses was again favorable. Liberals everywhere cheered the president. The unofficial response was highly enthusiastic in England. After the armistice, Lloyd George also spoke on the same themes and similarly emphasized the importance of a league of nations. Thus, although there were no formal conferences and agreements, a large degree of Anglo-American harmony on essential war aims had been realized. Wilson also had become, informally but indisputably, the spokesman of the Allied and Associated states. His "drum-fire" speeches have been credited by some authorities with considerable success in driving a wedge between the German people and their rulers. Recent reevaluations have indicated, however, that there was no noticeable effect until the German government made the first overture for an armistice. Only then, when Germany obviously faced military defeat, did the seeds of distrust and disillusionment with the war, stimulated by Wilson's speeches, produce overt results.

Wilson's idealistic pronouncements probably had little lasting effect on most Americans. They were more likely to be affected by emotional appeals to crush the enemy than by abstract concepts of a just peace and a league of nations. As House recorded

---

[11] *Congressional Record*, 65th Congress, 2d Session, Vol. 56, 4757–4758.

in his diary, after hearing the president's address at the Metropolitan Opera House on September 27: "Most of it seemed somewhat over the heads of his audience, the parts which were unimportant bringing the most vigorous applause." [12] Perhaps heavier emphasis on the practical value for America of the new world order would have been advisable, in view of the subsequent disillusionment, but such an approach would have been foreign to Wilson's psychology and his concept of his role. Furthermore, many of his pronouncements of principles were overgeneralized. That avoided immediate difficulties with the Allied governments but it created some popular misconceptions. Thus, for example, the reference to open or democratic diplomacy were popularly interpreted to mean that henceforth diplomats should operate in the full glare of publicity. This was not what Wilson meant, as he wrote Lansing, for it would make diplomacy virtually impossible: "I meant not that there should be no private discussions of delicate matters, but that no secret agreements of any sort should be entered into and that all international relations, when fixed, should be open, above-board, and explicit." [13] As one Wilson student has concluded, the Fourteen Points and other addresses were sufficently vague and idealistic for war propaganda purposes, but in many particulars were inadequate for peacemaking.

IV

The Wilsonian slogan of self-determination has been held responsible by some critics for the Balkanization of Europe after World War I. His pronouncements actually had less effect, save that of a quickening of events, in the emergence of a number of new states from the shattered Austrian, German, and Russian empires. Nationalism was not a creation of the author of the Fourteen Points address, and it had been one of the obvious causes of the outbreak of war in 1914. The peace treaty, if it

---

[12] Seymour, *Intimate Papers*, IV, 71.

[13] Wilson to Lansing, March 12, 1918, *Foreign Relations, Lansing Papers*, II, 112–113.

were to have any prospects for permanence, would have to recognize nationalistic aspirations and to satisfy at least the larger ones. In recognizing that fact in his various statements of war goals, Wilson was being practical as well as idealistic.

President Wilson at first had believed that the unity of the Austro-Hungarian empire should be preserved if possible, apparently because dissolution would create a dangerous power vacuum in eastern and central Europe. In early 1917, after the diplomatic break with Germany, Wilson had tried to detach Austria from the war by securing Allied assurances against dismemberment. Diplomatic relations, consequently, were not immediately severed with Vienna despite Austria's concurrence in the U-boat campaign. The efforts at detachment failed when the empire proved unable or unwilling to make peace without Germany. When the United States entered the war in April, the Austro-Hungarian government severed diplomatic relations with America. Not until December 1917, after urgent Allied requests for increased aid to Italy in the aftermath of the military disaster at Caporetto, did the American government belatedly declare war against the Austrian empire. Even so, in his war message Wilson disavowed any intention to dismember the monarchy.

In the Fourteen Points address Wilson advocated in Point 10 the fullest opportunity for autonomous development (within the empire) of the peoples of Austria-Hungary. He had begun to move away from his earlier position because of growing awareness of the dissatisfied Slavic nationalities within the empire, to whom he desired to appeal in order to put additional pressure on the imperial government to withdraw from the war. Secretary Lansing had for some time been convinced that nothing less than the total dismemberment of the multinational empire would suffice. Albert Putney of the State Department's Near Eastern Division had drafted memoranda which recommended a peace settlement in central and eastern Europe along nationality lines, with the creation of Yugoslav, Polish, and Czech states, as just and as the expedient way to erect strong barriers against German ambition and expansion. Convinced of the soundness of such a course, Lansing viewed Wilson's Point 10 as unfortunate in its continued support of a federal Austrian empire. The January 8 speech also caused distress in Italy. Wilson's

reference to Italian boundaries based on clear lines of nationality conflicted with Italy's ambitions for expansion along the
Adriatic Sea, in areas not necessarily inhabited by a majority
of Italians.

By May, Lansing had concluded that it was desirable to make
a definite policy statement about the nationalities within the
Viennese empire. "It is my judgment that, primarily as a war-
measure, and also because it is just and wise for the future, we
should encourage in every possible way the national desires of
these peoples." [14] Because Austria-Hungary was so bound to
Germany as to preclude a separate peace, he inquired of Wilson
if it would not be a wise war measure to support self-determination for the Slavic peoples within the empire. Wilson apparently was impressed with the force of the secretary's analysis
and he conferred with him on the subject at the White House.
He agreed that a change in policy was advisable but asked
Lansing first to approach Italy on the problem. The Italian government approved recognition of the Czechoslovak movement
as a means to weaken the enemy, but, as Lansing cynically
commented, was unenthusiastic about the Yugoslavs because
of its conflicting interests with Serbia: "It is all after a piece
with the selfish policy which wrecked the Balkan situation early
in the war." [15] In Lansing's opinion, the Yugloslavs (Serbians
plus the other South Slavs then under Austrian jurisdiction)
were a sufficiently well-defined nationality to merit support
regardless of Italian opposition.

With Wilson's agreement, a carefully drawn policy statement
was released by Lansing on May 29, 1918, which declared
American sympathy with the nationalistic desires of the Yugoslavs and Czechoslovaks. The motive rather clearly was a
matter of war expediency, to weaken the Central powers and
hasten their collapse. A secondary factor was the conviction
that creation of these new states would be just and would help
stabilize central Europe in the future by checking pan-German

---

[14] "Memorandum on Our Policy in Relation to Austria-Hungary," May 30,
1918, Private Memoranda, Lansing Papers.

[15] Lansing to Wilson, May 21, 1918, *Foreign Relations, Lansing Papers*, II,
129–130.

ambitions. Time was to raise serious questions about the latter assumption, as the states carved out of Austria-Hungary proved unequal in the 1930's to the challenge of a revived Germany. That result was not inevitable, however, for a firmer French and British attitude in 1936–1938 probably would have created an entirely different situation.

The final blow to the integrity of the Austrian empire came in June when Wilson approved a Lansing memorandum for a policy sanctioning complete dismemberment. A further statement was made to the Serbian government and in September the belligerency of the Czechoslovak Council and army was recognized. In neither case, however, were commitments made as to boundaries, for both Wilson and Lansing agreed upon the necessity of "keeping ourselves free for [the] peace treaty." [16]

Polish groups, like the Czechs and others, were also active in the United States trying to arouse support among compatriots who had immigrated to America and to secure recognition and aid from the Washington authorities. Apparently the immigrant groups had little direct influence on Wilson's policy but the organized councils did enjoy some success in their efforts. The United States supported Polish independence for approximately the same reasons as in the case of the Czechs and South Slavs. The War Department permitted Polish nationals to enlist in Polish armies and the Polish National Council in Paris was dealt with as the unofficial representative of the Polish nation. In point 13 of the Fourteen Points, Wilson supported the establishment of a new Poland based on clear nationality principles. In November 1918 a recognition of cobelligerency was extended to the Polish Council.

These new states were not created by the United States or by the Paris Peace Conference. In effect, they were already in existence by the time the conference met, and largely as the inevitable result of the collapse of the Germanic and Russian empires. American policy had stimulated and encouraged the process of dissolution of the multinational Austro-Hungarian empire and the emergence of the "succession states" as neces-

---

[16] August 30, 1918, Lansing Desk Diary.

sary war measures and for the purpose of promoting a more stable and secure Europe. Idealism and realistic considerations were thereby harmonized in American policy.

V

By the fall of 1918 Germany's military leaders were compelled to recognize that all hope for victory was gone. In western Europe, Germany confronted growing Allied strength as American troops and supplies arrived in vast numbers. The Allied generalissimo, Marshal Ferdinand Foch, had successfully parried the last German drives and had launched a powerful counteroffensive, while Germany's allies, Turkey, Bulgaria, and Austria-Hungary, were beginning to collapse and to seek peace. Field Marshal Hindenburg and General Ludendorff of the high command experienced near panic and a loss of nerve in September and peremptorily requested the civilian government under the new chancellor, Prince Max von Baden, to sue for an immediate armistice. Ludendorff, the strategic intelligence behind the imposing facade of Hindenburg, apparently hoped for a pause in hostilities which would permit his armies to retire in orderly fashion and to regroup along the Rhine River; from that position Germany either could negotiate for a peace on a basis of near equality with the enemy or resume the war if necessary and fight on for better terms. Prince Max's government consequently addressed a request to President Wilson on October 4 for a peace based on the principles announced in his Fourteen Points speech and in other addresses.

A period of mounting tension and delicate diplomacy ensued. With consummate skill, indicating again his ability to fuse ideals and reality, Wilson avoided the German diplomatic traps and probably hastened the conclusion of the war by at least several months. News of the German peace overture aroused much concern in the Allied camp lest the wily enemy deceive the presumably naive idealist in the White House and escape with milder terms than were desirable. The anxious Allied governments were not directly informed of Wilson's plans in replying and they feared that Allied military supremacy might be compromised by the president. In the United States, where the war temper had reached an alarming intensity and many normally responsible people were advocating the complete crushing of Germany and the imposition of a harsh peace, voices were raised in Congress and the press in apprehension that Wilson would consent to a premature armistice and to soft terms of peace. The exasperated president exclaimed on one occasion, "Do they think I am a damned fool?" [17]

The fears were unnecessary. Wilson skillfully continued the exchange with Berlin until German civilian and army morale disintegrated and the German authorities had no option but to accept armistice terms which precluded a resumption of the war. Wilson's first reply, on October 8, was drafted without consultation with the Allies and inquired if Germany accepted unequivocally the Fourteen and related points as the basis of peace. An immediate evacuation of Belgian and French territory was requested and the president indicated his desire to deal only with a civilian government truly representative of the German people. The second German note to Wilson was received on October 14 and, although it made clear a complete acceptance of the Fourteen Points and asserted that Prince Max's government was representative of the German nation, it suggested the creation of a joint belligerent commission to arrange the details of evacuation. The Allied governments viewed that proposal as a device to arrange for a slow and orderly withdrawal that would leave the German army intact and in a good defensive position to continue the war. Two notes were therefore sent by the Allied premiers to Wilson, which emphasized that evacuation of occupied territory was not sufficient and that the details of an armistice should be left to the military advisers in order to preserve the existing supremacy of the Allied military forces. Wilson was then requested to send a representative to Europe to engage in the formulation of military terms. The president's second reply to Berlin was carefully phrased to avoid the German snare. The note of October 14 rejected the proposed mixed commission and made it clear that

---

[17] Arthur Walworth, *Woodrow Wilson* (New York: Longmans, Green, 1958, 2 vols.), II, 188.

the details of evacuation and armistice would be left to the determination of the military experts of the Allied and Associated powers.

There was a strengthened conviction within the American government that the Hohenzollern dynasty should be toppled if a lasting peace was to be achieved. Throughout the war Wilson had repeatedly drawn a distinction between the presumably basically decent and peaceful German people and their autocratic and militaristic rulers. Kaiser Wilhelm II, with his fierce-appearing moustaches and his penchant for military trappings, symbolized the hated Junker oligarchy and throughout America was viewed virtually as the incarnation of evil. His abdication alone would not suffice, however, for he would only be succeeded by one of his sons. As Secretary Lansing commented to the press about rumors of the emperor's abdication, only "if he should abdicate in favor of a democratic Germany [would] it . . . mean something." [18] Subsequently Lansing strongly recommended to the president that the kaiser and his dynasty would have to be eliminated as "a guarantee of [German] good faith." [19] Wilson probably needed no urging. His note of October 14 had referred to the arbitrary character of the German government and again intimated the desirability of a change.

The German civilian officials found themselves in a dilemma, with the army high command now preferring a continuation of the war rather than accepting a humiliating armistice amounting to surrender, while the rumors of peace had so affected the war-weary German people as to make a continuation of hostilities virtually impossible. Ludendorff's objections were therefore ignored and on October 20 the government fully accepted Wilson's terms, although once more insisting that the present German cabinet was representative of the people. The Allied leaders were increasingly hesitant about a peace based on the Fourteen Points and Wilson was again requested to leave the Armistice details to the experts. The president had no intention of usurping authority to reach a bilateral armistice agreement with Germany, and on October 23 he informed the Berlin

---

[18] October 11, 1918, *New York Times.*
[19] October 23, 1918, Lansing Desk Diary.

regime that he was submitting the correspondence to the Allied governments with the recommendation that armistice terms should be promptly prepared. Since he repeated his questioning of the democratic character of the German government, and since revolutionary fervor mounted in Germany itself, the sequel was the forced abdication of Wilhelm II and his dynasty on November 9.

There is little doubt that Wilson had consciously sought the creation of a republic in Germany. House apparently felt less strongly on that point and viewed a limited or constitutional monarchy as satisfactory. But the general temper in America, as well as among most of Wilson's close advisers, would have viewed any settlement which left the monarchy intact, even if only a facade, as a betrayal of the ideological goals of the war. Wilson must have agreed. After he had replied to the last German note and while Colonel House was hurrying to Europe for the armistice discussions, Secretary Lansing instructed the America *chargé* at The Hague to let it be known that a current report that Wilson would not insist on the kaiser's abdication was completely unwarranted and should not be given credence. Historian Thomas A. Bailey has pointed out that the German people received the impression that the peace would be easier with Wilhelm's elimination, as a national scapegoat, and they subsequently felt betrayed when the victorious powers still insisted on holding the German nation fully responsible for the war. It is difficult, however, to envision a feasible alternative granted the wartime psychology in America and Europe. Hindsight suggests, as Bailey notes, that it probably would have been wiser to have forced the kaiser's government to remain in power long enough to shoulder the responsibility for losing the war and for acceptance of an unpopular peace treaty. Then perhaps a subsequent German republic, had it occurred, would have had a better prospect of stability than was the one established after the kaiser's abdication.

As for later German charges, especially by Adolf Hitler, that the German armies were unbeaten in 1918 and had been "stabbed in the back" by the civilians, the evidence is clear that the army had in fact been defeated and that the anxiety of Hindenburg and Ludendorff in September had compelled the civilian government to begin peace discussions with Wilson. The president's able handling of the exchanges and the resultant deterioration of civilian and military morale in Germany thus brought the war to an end months in advance of predictions by the experts. Thousands of lives and millions of dollars were probably saved, and even greater chaos in Europe averted. Finally, the Allies were still free to act if they had decided that it would be desirable to continue the war and invade Germany. Wilson had no doubt made such a decision hard to defend, but it was at least still within the realm of possibility.

The next phase of the armistice negotiations began with Colonel House's arrival at Paris to represent the United States at the sessions of the Supreme War Council. Wilson very realistically wanted the terms to be sufficiently strong to prevent renewal of the war but yet to leave Germany with enough force-in-being to serve as a counterpoise to excessive Allied ambitions. As he wrote House on October 28, the armistice terms should preclude a resumption of the war but not leave the Allies feeling so secure as to make a genuine peace settlement impossible. House's mission was to obtain Allied acceptance of the Fourteen Points as the basis for the peace to be offered Germany. He performed this task with considerable skill and success.

The Supreme War Council agreed upon naval and military terms which made it difficult if not impossible for a resumption of hostilities by Germany. German armies were to be withdrawn immediately to the Rhine River and were to turn over to the Allies large amounts of war materiel, airplanes, artillery, and machine guns; 160 submarines were to be surrendered as well, and the largest part of the navy was to be interned in a British port. In the discussions of the Fourteen Points as the contract for peace, however, greater difficulty was experienced.

The Allied governments in general were unenthusiastic about adopting the Fourteen Points as the basis for peace. The several secret treaties and agreements previously made envisioned a different type of settlement with the Central powers. Consequently blanket endorsement of the Wilsonian pronouncements was refused and a point-by-point discussion was insisted upon. Great Britain took exception to Point 2 concerning the freedom of the seas. A memorandum prepared by Walter Lippmann and Frank Cobb, and used by House to explain the meaning of the Fourteen Points, defined freedom of the seas as full observance by belligerents of neutral rights in a future war which was not in contravention to international agreements. The British government viewed this principle as in effect nullifying the advantages of sea power by conferring the power of blockade on an untried league of nations, and to a large extent immunizing private property from capture on the high seas. Sharp exchanges occurred between Lloyd George and House, and the latter threatened that if Point 2 were not adopted the United States probably would have to build a much larger navy to protect its commerce. House also declared that if the Allies nullified or rejected the Fourteen Points, Wilson might have to request Congress to approve a separate treaty of peace. The president cabled his approval of House's action. If the Allied leaders sought to nullify his influence in advance of the peace conference, Wilson told the colonel, he was prepared to confront them squarely and to challenge selfish proposals openly. In addition to British objections, France desired to define Point 8 on the restoration of evacuated territory to specify payment for damages done by the enemy to all civilian property. After further acrimonious discussion it was finally agreed to accept the Fourteen Points with two qualifications, one embodying the French definition of the restoration of invaded areas and damaged property, and the other a British reservation that the principle of freedom of the seas should be fully and freely discussed at the peace conference. Italian and Belgian objections and reservations were then brushed aside and the so-called Pre-Armistice Agreement was completed. On November 5 President Wilson communicated to Germany the agreement of the Allied and Associated powers to grant a peace based on the Fourteen Points with two reservations, and the German authorities were directed to send representatives to receive the military terms of the armistice. The armistice was signed on November 11 and a few hours later over four years of incredibly bloody warfare came to a halt.

The Pre-Armistice Agreement was a triumph for Wilson and House. It was not a victory imposed on Great Britain, however, for Lloyd George's war addresses had also enunciated a liberal peace and on Point 2, the freedom of the seas, full freedom for subsequent debate had been reserved. Ironically, when the peace conference did meet, the overriding importance which Wilson attached to the League of Nations and its economic and military sanctions to preserve peace and punish aggression made neutrality issues relatively unimportant and the question of freedom of the seas was not revived. As for France, it also had secured a reservation to the Fourteen Points on the important question of war damages. Other powers at the Supreme War Council had indicated that they too would question details of the application of Wilsonian ideals at the peace negotiations. Clemenceau is said once to have remarked cynically, "God gave us the Ten Commandments, and we broke them. Wilson gives us the Fourteen Points. We shall see." [20] Yet Wilson had at least won a formal if grudging Allied assent to peace based on his principles and he no doubt was justified in assuming that the secret treaties were thereby either nullified or relegated to a secondary place. On the eve of the convening of the greatest peace conference since the Congress of Vienna in 1815, President Wilson could take great satisfaction in having contributed decisively to military victory over Germany and in an equally important diplomatic triumph in formulating the bases for the peace.

---

[20] As quoted in William Allen White, *Woodrow Wilson: the Man, His Times, and His Task* (Boston: Houghton Mifflin, 1924), 384.

CHAPTER VII

A Victory for Collective Security

A S THE WAR NEARED AN END, Wilson prepared for a supreme
effort to achieve a liberal peace. Despite errors and compromises at the Paris Peace Conference, he was to help secure a
treaty which was reasonable in its principal provisions and which
above all embodied what he regarded as the crowning goal, the
Covenant of the League of Nations. Unfortunately, Wilson
gave insufficient attention to the domestic front in the United
States and his handiwork was to be rejected by the Senate.

I

Several decisions made by President Wilson as the war
ended were to weaken his position at the peace conference.
One was his appeal to the voters to return Democratic ma-
jorities to Congress in the fall elections of 1918. Endorsement
of the Democratic Party by the electorate would indicate popular approval of the administration on the eve of the peace conference, he announced, and would strengthen him for the
crucial work ahead; but "The return of a Republican majority
. . . would . . . certainly be interpreted on the other side of
the water as a repudiation of my leadership." [1] Wilson had
hesitated about the appeal — a number of his cabinet members
advised   against it — but finally capitulated to the pleas of
Democratic officeholders and politicians for support in a close
election. The Republicans, normally the majority party, were

---

[1] Ray Stannard Baker and William E. Dodd, *The Public Papers of Woodrow
Wilson: War and Peace* (New York: Harper, 1927, 2 vols.), I, 286–288.

exploiting growing popular discontent with the privations and restrictions imposed by the war, and Democratic congressmen from marginal districts anxiously requested White House aid. An additional motive, no doubt, was Wilson's predilection for a parliamentary system and his tendency to view the presidency as evolving toward a type of prime ministership.

During the war, politics presumably had been adjourned as both parties rallied to support of the war effort. Nevertheless, Wilson had found his administration under sharp attack for alleged inefficiency in mobilizing the national energies and resources for the war on Germany and he had had to rebuff several attempts by Republican critics to compel formation of a coalition cabinet or creation of a joint committee to direct the national mobilization. Unfortunately, Wilson's appeal allowed his opponents to accuse him of being excessively partisan and with impugning the loyal service of opposition congressmen.

When the returns revealed a Republican victory in both houses of Congress, Republican spokesmen promptly claimed that Wilson had requested a popular vote of confidence in his leadership and had lost. Some political opponents, such as Theodore Roosevelt, openly declared that Wilson had been repudiated by the electorate and no longer could speak for the American nation. Roosevelt's bitter hatred of Wilson undoubtedly explained his outburst, for he must have known that midterm congressional elections often are adverse for the party in power and that they usually reflect only local issues. The 1918 canvass obviously was not a national mandate on Wilson's leadership and under the Constitution he would continue as the sole official spokesman on foreign affairs for the United States.

In defense of Wilson's appeal to the voters it is possible that his intervention actually reduced Democratic losses. Even if he had remained silent, Republican victories would still have had an adverse impact abroad. Yet to have explicitly called for a vote of confidence made the results more dramatic and serious, and undoubtedly diminished the president's strength at the forthcoming negotiations. The leaders of the major Allied states were to meet him at Paris after winning popular elections or renewed parliamentary mandates. Hindsight thus indicates that

Wilson made an understandable error, for he would probably have lost less in prestige and influence if he had remained more aloof in the election.

Soon after the election, critics of the administration were furnished additional ammunition when the names of the American plenipotentiaries to negotiate the peace were announced. The White House revealed that the president would personally attend the peace conference and that he would be assisted by Secretary of State Lansing, Colonel House, General Tasker H. Bliss, and Henry White as fellow Commissioners Plenipotentiary. General Bliss was an able soldier with an intelligent interest and knowledge in economic and political affairs; White, a minor Republican but an experienced diplomat, was selected primarily upon Lansing's recommendation. Lansing, by virtue of his position, could hardly have been left off the commission, despite Wilson's growing coolness toward him. House undoubtedly was one of the ablest of the delegation and at Paris was to make one of the most favorable impressions on the Allied leaders. European observers generally agreed that he was the most capable diplomat among the Americans. Yet news of the composition of the delegation caused critics to condemn Wilson's personal attendance as unprecedented and as an indication of his egotistical desire to bask in the limelight of Paris and to dominate the writing of the peace. He was accused of having a messiah complex, of believing that only he could achieve a good peace treaty. As for his fellow commissioners, a torrent of criticism was aroused because Wilson had allegedly appointed only weak or subservient men. Why, it was asked, had no prominent Republicans been named, and no members of the Senate from either party?

The elder Republican statesman, Elihu Root, reflected the views of many that Wilson's proper place was at home to supervise domestic affairs and that he should have let Lansing head the delegation. Root shared the belief of a number of other Wilsonian critics, Republican and Democratic as well, that the president was an autocrat bordering on egomania. He remarked to Chandler P. Anderson that Wilson would probably be more interested in establishing an international league executive than a world court, because he expected himself to be "the universal choice for the president of the world." [2] Ex-President Taft exclaimed, upon learning of the makeup of the commission, that the whole group was "a cheap lot of skates. I could swear if it would do any good." [3] The angry reaction of many Republicans to Wilson was perhaps best summed up in a political joke then current in Washington. "Wilsonitis" was a new disease, "the symptoms of which are the placing of the reasoning powers in cold storage, and applauding anything which Woodrow Wilson might do, irrespective of the merits thereof." [4]

The president's decision to attend the conference had also been opposed by several members of the administration. Secretary Lansing had braved Wilson's wrath to advise that it would be a mistake, for at Paris he would presumably lose his commanding stature by being compelled to bargain intimately with his equals, whereas if he remained in America he not only would escape Republican criticism but could control the conference from afar. Colonel House, then in Paris after the armistice negotiations, obliquely indicated his opposition by reporting that the Allied leaders were opposed to the president's attendance as a delegate, among other reasons because Wilson alone would be a head of state and the resultant protocol problems would be great. The colonel apparently believed himself best fitted for the delicate task of negotiation and he did not view Wilson as excelling in a situation where he was forced to cope with equals. Wilson tartly replied that most Americans wanted and expected him to attend, which was hardly an accurate appraisal, and that he regarded opposition as indicative of Allied intentions to curtail his influence for a just peace. British and French obstructionism, which indeed reflected apprehension that the American president would try to dominate the peace-making, thus foundered on the rock of Wilsonian obduracy. Others, such as Secretary of War Newton D. Baker, concurred

---

[2] November 18, 1918, Chandler P. Anderson Diary, Library of Congress.

[3] Henry F. Pringle, *The Life and Times of William Howard Taft* (New York: Farrar & Rinehart, 1939, 2 vols.), II, 941.

[4] Anderson Diary.

that attendance by Wilson was inadvisable. Lansing, no doubt not unwilling himself to head the delegation but genuinely concerned over the ill effects if Wilson attended, asked Vance McCormick to try to dissuade the president. After McCormick had raised the question, Wilson inquired who would go as chief of the mission if he did not: "Lansing is not big enough. House won't do. Taft and Root are not in sympathy with our plans. I must go." [5]

Probably Wilson was wise in rejecting such negative advice. He could not have relied upon Lansing, who was out of sympathy with many of his plans, and House's tendency toward compromise and conciliation subsequently aroused his intense annoyance at Paris. No doubt he should have been more concerned about the political temper of Congress and the nation. As John A. Garraty has pointed out, Wilson's advisers would have been on sounder grounds if they had objected that he was needed at home to keep the Senate favorable to ratification of whatever should be achieved at the peace conference. Against that consideration was Wilson's conviction that he had an overriding moral obligation to the people of the world to battle for a treaty based on the Fourteen Points. He was supremely confident that no one else could do this as well and that he, more than the Allied leaders, spoke for American and Allied public opinion. In retrospect it seems that his assessment was at least partly correct. The resultant peace settlement was much better for Wilson's presence and valiant efforts. Whatever his mistakes, Wilson "emerges as the only man of real stature at Paris." [6]

Less defensible, however, was the president's failure to appoint a major Republican figure or a member of the Senate to the peace commission. When the names of prominent pro-league Republicans, such as Charles Evans Hughes and Taft, were suggested to him as suitable commissioners whose presence would make the peacemaking a nonpolitical or bipartisan ven-

---

[5] As quoted by Vance McCormick, McCormick Interview, Ray Stannard Baker Papers, Library of Congress.

[6] Paul Birdsall, *Versailles Twenty Years After* (New York: Reynal & Hitchcock, 1941), 294–295.

ture, Wilson conveniently found reasons to reject them. Hughes and Taft, he asserted, were not in sympathy with his ideas, and he dismissed Root as hopelessly reactionary. Suggestions that one or two senators be named, as McKinley had done in 1898, were rejected by him on the rather thin grounds that it was constitutionally improper to ask senators to participate in drafting a treaty which the whole Senate would subsequently have to consider.

The true reason for Wilson's refusal to appoint a major Republican leader or members of the Senate undoubtedly must be found within his personal psychology. He was highly ambitious and morally certain of his own rectitude. Once he had concluded that a particular course was demanded by considerations of principle, his entire being was committed and he tended to view any criticism as either indicative of disloyalty to him personally or as revealing ignorance and stupidity on the part of the critic. By the fall of 1918 he was almost consumed with his sacred mission to achieve a moral peace settlement capped by a constitution for the world, the League of Nations Covenant. He was increasingly inflexible, determined to dominate the peace conference to achieve *his* peace and then to force it upon a perhaps rebellious Senate. The thought of taking powerful and independent individuals, such as Hughes or Taft, to Paris where they might well object to aspects of his program or his leadership was highly unpalatable to the president. In regard to senators, if he had named a Republican it would probably have had to be Henry Cabot Lodge of Massachusetts, whom he personally disliked. As he remarked to the Czech leader, Thomas G. Masaryk, the presence of such men would necessitate the compromising of differences within the American delegation, for which he had no heart: "I tell you frankly, I am descended from Scottish Presbyterians and am therefore somewhat stubborn." [7]

The error, for such it proved to be, was compounded by Wilson's failure to consult the Senate, either the leaders of both parties or the Foreign Relations Committee, on the problems likely to arise at the peace negotiations. There was little precedent for such consultation, however, even though the effort

---

[7] Walworth, *Woodrow Wilson*, II, 211.

might well have conciliated some senators and have reduced opposition to Wilson's league plans. Instead he addressed a joint session of Congress on December 2, two days prior to his departure for Europe. Before the rather sullen Republicans in the assemblage, he defended his attendance at the Paris conference as necessary to interpret the Fourteen Points on which the armistice was based: the Allied governments, he disingenuously declared, "very reasonably desire my personal counsel in their interpretation and application." Wilson closed with the expressed hope for the encouragement and support of Congress in his "efforts truly and faithfully to interpret the principles and purposes of the country we love. . . ." [8] Since he had not consulted Congress or indicated in any detail what he proposed to achieve, it was understandable that many Republicans and some Democrats listened without enthusiasm to his exhortation. These acts of commission and omission by Wilson increased the probability that the Senate would challenge his leadership in foreign affairs and that the peace treaty would become a partisan issue.

II

On the morning of December 4 the president boarded the *S. S. George Washington* for the voyage to Europe, accompanied by members of the peace commission and experts from the Inquiry, with numerous studies and maps. The great ship departed a few hours later, to the accompaniment of circling planes and salutes from other ships in the harbor; the great adventure was underway. The crossing was uneventful, although already some of Wilson's fellow commissioners began to complain of the president's vagueness and uncommunicativeness about plans for the settlement. In one very revealing statement, however, Wilson told the assembled experts that at Paris the Americans would be the only disinterested group and would be confronting Allied spokesmen who did not truly represent the desires of their own people. A league of nations was mandatory, he asserted, as

---

[8] *Congressional Record*, 65th Congress, 3rd Session, Vol. 57, 5–8.

the indispensable means to guarantee the peace and independence of all states and to correct any inequities which might be embodied in other parts of the treaty. Thus the league would provide both security and elasticity, the very antithesis of archaic balances of power. He closed the interview with an appeal to the assembled scholars to tell him what was right at Paris and he would fight for it with all his energy.

Wilson's remarks indicated not only that he was convinced of the central importance of a league of nations but that he was laboring under several serious delusions as he approached the conference. The Allied leaders were not unprincipled, even if they did speak for more materialistic national interests than did Wilson. Britain and France particularly had paid a great price for survival in the war and necessarily their leaders, especially the French, were concerned with safeguards for the future. Furthermore, the great majority of their people did in fact endorse their plans for achieving security and retribution from the defeated enemy. Wilson represented a country which had paid a very small price comparatively for national security and therefore had few concrete demands to make at Paris. The Allied leaders regarded the noble American goals as a luxury possible only because the Allies had borne the brunt of the war and had served as a protective shield for the United States. Wilson was to discover painfully that these leaders, and not himself, represented only too well the desires of their people for a vindictive peace.

The peace conference did not begin its deliberations until nearly a month after the Americans arrived. The delay no doubt was tragic, in view of the general chaos in central Europe and the need for a quick peace to raise the blockade and restore normal conditions. Germany was seething with revolt; the Austro-Hungarian empire had disintegrated and new turbulent states were emerging; Russia was in civil war, and the virus of Bolshevism seemed daily to flourish on the widespread hunger and despair. It took time, however, to assemble the delegates of the thirty-two great and small powers at Paris, to secure quarters, and to organize the conference physically. In addition there was an understandable lethargy after long years of war, as western Europe prepared to enjoy its first postwar Christmas holiday.

President Wilson utilized the interval to visit England and Italy where his receptions generally were enthusiastic and often tumultuous. Paris welcomed him first with a parade and crowds unequaled in the memory of observers; the English reception was perhaps a little less demonstrative but nonetheless flattering and amply satisfying; and Rome's greeting was a delirium of shouting, weeping, and cheering crowds hailing the messiah from the west. Wilson could hardly avoid the conviction that he was the voice of world opinion, that he represented the instincts of the masses for an equitable peace. Perhaps reflection should have suggested to him that there probably was a very wide discrepancy between the popular concept of a just peace and his own ideas. The president also managed to anger some by his reluctance to praise publicly the gallantry of the British and Allied soldiers in the war or to visit battlefields and cemeteries. His refusal, based on the desire to remain dispassionate for the task ahead, was most creditable but impolitic.

The conference, which finally began work on January 12, has been described as a kind of order within chaos. The atmosphere was frenzied and feverish, with milling delegates, anxious representatives of small powers requesting favors, spokesmen of minority and ethnic groups seeking special treatment, and the ubiquitous and usually frustrated members of the press. Officially the assembly was known as the Preliminary Peace Conference, for the German delegates did not participate until May 7 when the formal peace conference briefly came into being. The preliminary conference theoretically was controlled by the plenary sessions of all the participating powers. In practice, it was dominated by the great powers — France, Great Britain, the United States, Italy, and, to a limited degree, Japan. The Big Four of Wilson, Clemenceau, Lloyd George, and Vittorio Orlando (of Italy) carried on the most important work of the conference, at first through the Council of Ten (chiefs of state and premiers with their foreign ministers), and subsequently in the Council of Four. Under the Council of Ten were sixty commissions, established to deal with the specific problems of territorial, economic, and military settlements. Contrary to their expectations, the numerous reporters discovered that "open covenants openly arrived at" did not mean full freedom to cover the deliberations but only the receipt of prepared short news releases and the coverage of the rare and usually arid formal plenary sessions of the conference. President Wilson wanted a more generous policy but was overruled by the other leaders. Many Americans promptly came to the erroneous conclusion that one of the Fourteen Points had been violated at the outset of the peace conference.

Wilson was preeminent among the leaders of the great powers at Paris in terms of detailed knowledge and his great efforts to comprehend and solve intelligently the various problems which arose. He was courteous and usually patient in relations with the other leaders and seldom displayed annoyance at their delays and endless maneuvering. Wilson listened closely to the discussions in the councils and commissions and expended much energy in an effort to master the complexities of every problem. He thereby placed a great strain on his already frail physique. Lloyd George, however, impressed observers with his rather imperturbable ignorance and erratic behavior. He was an able and magnetic politician who apparently operated without a plan. His opportunism probably has been exaggerated — on the whole he advocated a reasonable settlement at Paris and agreed with Wilson on most basic issues — but he was able to reverse course with amazing equanimity. Lansing aptly depicted Lloyd George as notable rather for the alertness than for the profundity of his mind. Without the aid of his able foreign secretary, Arthur J. Balfour, it was generally agreed that the British premier would have been decidedly outclassed in the council chambers at Paris. In general, Lloyd George sought to meliorate the treatment of Germany lest future war-breeding Alsace-Lorraines be created and valuable British markets in Germany lost. Undoubtedly he also hoped to avoid an undue enhancement of French dominance on the continent. Only in regard to the issues of reparations and disposal of the German colonies did he depart noticeably from a moderate course. Clemenceau, the French premier, was nearly eighty years of age and often dozed during conference discussions of little importance to France. Stooped, white haired, with a jutting jaw and drooping moustaches, Clemenceau was popularly nicknamed "The Tiger." A realist and a cynic, his central aim at the conference was revenge on Germany and security for a war-weakened France. Lansing described him as nearly Oriental in appearance: "He was a striking type, indicative of intellectual force, of self-mastery, and of cold, merciless will power. . . . [H]e watched the course of events with Oriental stoicism and calculated with . . . unerring instinct . . . the interests of France. . . ." [9] Clemenceau was often puzzled by Wilson's idealism and apparently viewed him with an ironic condescension. The last of the Big Four, Italian Premier Orlando, impressed Lansing and other observers as an able, realistic, and usually moderate political leader. He alone among the Big Four leaders could not speak English and his role was largely restricted to aspects of the treaty directly affecting Italy.

The criticism so often raised during and after the conference that Wilson lacked preparation at Paris and failed to consult others was only partly valid. The Inquiry, as noted before, had labored diligently to prepare materials on the principal questions to be considered at the conference. At Paris, Wilson apparently utilized extensively both these reports and the service of the experts he had brought to Europe. He was seldom, if ever, deceived or confused by the Allied leaders and usually had the firmest grasp of the problems under consideration.

Unfortunately, however, Wilson generally neglected his fellow commissioners, with the exception of Colonel House. Lansing, Bliss, and White were rarely consulted or informed by the president and were often reduced to gleaning information from the British delegation about the progress of the Big Four. Lansing, a lawyer by training, had wanted to prepare a skeleton treaty for the guidance of the American delegation but Wilson brushed him aside with the curt and insulting remark that "he did not intend to have lawyers drafting the treaty of peace." [10] As a result there was a certain lack of central direction and coordination among the American representatives, and to a degree the initiative and the machinery of the conference consequently were left in French hands. Adoption of a detailed treaty plan would have made possible a greater consistency of effort in framing

---

[9] Robert Lansing, *The Big Four and Others of the Peace Conference* (Boston: Houghton Mifflin, 1921), 33.

[10] Robert Lansing, *The Peace Negotiations, A Personal Narrative* (Boston: Houghton Mifflin, 1921), 107.

the terms of the various settlements. It was only in this limited way, however, that Wilson can correctly be accused of lack of a program at Paris. The relative neglect of the commissioners (they were of course active in some of the work of the conference) was doubly unfortunate, for they were men of talent whose fuller utilization could have relieved Wilson of some of his burdens and probably would have contributed to some improvement in the completed treaty. Apparently the president was absorbed by his plans for the League and in any case he preferred to work in solitary concentration without trying to persuade his fellow commissioners. In addition he was annoyed at Lansing's efforts to organize the delegation, had less and less confidence in his abilities, and received with ill-concealed hostility the secretary's suggestions for a different kind of league.

Colonel House at first basked in Wilson's confidence and played an important part in the conference. He took an obviously condescending attitude toward his less fortunate fellow plenipotentiaries. As he confided to his diary, "I feel embarrassed every day when I am with them." [11] He did urge the president, without notable success, to hold more conferences with the other three commissioners. Wilson rarely appeared at the regular meetings of the American delegation and House attended infrequently. Instead, Wilson often bypassed the rooms of Lansing, Bliss, and White in the Hotel Crillon enroute to House's suite, and the representatives of the Allies also frequented the colonel's apartment on affairs of high state. As a result of these snubs, and dissatisfaction with aspects of the settlements incorporated into the treaty, Lansing particularly became increasingly disgruntled and even considered not signing the treaty. Wilson was sufficiently concerned to have intermediaries approach the secretary to ensure that he would sign.

Lansing's wrath was especially aroused when, during Wilson's brief illness in April, House represented the president on the Council of Four. House at first continued his well-established techniques for managing the president and preserving his tenuous influence and power. No doubt with a note of bitterness Lansing,

---

[11] January 8, 1919, House Diary.

after a conference between the president and the other commissioners, recorded the secret of the colonel's success: "How well Col. House understands the President's character! He does not openly oppose him but endeavors to change him by putting his own interpretation on the President's words. The method seems to work, but I could not follow it. I cannot give the President the idea that I agree with him when I do not." [12] Yet slowly the Wilson-House relationship also cooled. House apparently was less flattering and subservient to the president than he had been in the past, and in his official position he often felt compelled to give Wilson criticism and painful advice. In additon it seems that Mrs. Wilson, long jealous of the role of the colonel, was affronted by the favorable publicity that House received as the "American prime minister," and that Wilson himself came to look sceptically on his intimate friend. The denouement was not a dramatic break but a gradual withdrawal by Wilson of his confidence in House. By June, as the German treaty was completed, House too was complaining bitterly to his fellow commissioners that he was unable to confer with the president privately and was uninformed about the activities of the Council of Four.

III

Despite lack of formal agreement or coordination, an Anglo-American community of interest generally prevailed at the Paris conference. A study by Seth P. Tillman of relations between the two states at Paris reveals that British and American goals were generally similar and that both governments usually supported adjustments that were moderate and that accorded with practical and idealistic considerations. At the highest level, President Wilson and Prime Minister Lloyd George did not establish an intimate rapport, because of strikingly different temperaments and Wilson's self-imposed isolation, but close if informal communication and cooperation existed between the other members of the two delegations. The consequent agreement on the essen-

---

[12] January 1, 1919, Appendix, Lansing Desk Diary.

tials of the peace contributed greatly to the more reasonable and progressive aspects of the final treaty with Germany.

One of the most important manifestations of Anglo-American harmony was the drafting of the Covenant of the League of Nations. Collective security through an international concert of power reflected the Anglo-American legalistic and constitutional tradition of government as one of laws and not of men and brute force. Since each country in the past had felt relatively secure and detached from the continental struggles for power, it had been comparatively easy to avoid the development of a militaristic tradition and to advocate the settlement of all serious international disputes by processes of conciliation and arbitration. Peace groups in both countries had been stimulated by World War I to develop the concept of an international organization which would encourage peaceful adjustments and prevent aggression. When British and American political figures became interested in the idea, French leaders conversely were less attracted and more sceptical unless somehow the idealistic proposal could be converted into an alliance of the victorious powers to preserve a new status quo favorable to French security and power. The charter achieved at Paris was the fruition of this movement and if the British were mainly responsible for the drafting of the concrete provisions of the League of Nations, Wilson preeminently was its sponsor and godfather.

After the American involvement in the war, Wilson resisted suggestions for an Anglo-American committee to draft a detailed plan for a league. The specifics of the league, he explained, should emerge more spontaneously and should evolve from democratic discussions and consultation. He envisioned the league as an organic growth and not as an artificial graft. A deeper reason for his refusal probably was his aversion to translating general principles into detailed arrangements, and perhaps a desire to control the process personally. Action was compelled, however, when the British war cabinet endorsed a plan in early 1918 known as the Phillimore Report. House warned Wilson that American and British opinion probably would crystallize around some unofficial or foreign scheme unless the president himself acted. As the colonel persuasively commented, such a result would be unfortunate, for the future league ought to be identified with the president's name as its chief architect.

After Wilson received a copy of the Phillimore Report, therefore, he directed the colonel to revise it in accordance with the ideas he and House had previously discussed. The Phillimore Report had suggested an alliance against nations which went to war in violation of procedures for the peaceful settlement of disputes. A subsequent draft, by Lord Robert Cecil, provided for a permanent council of the major powers to invoke sanctions. France also had a committee, headed by Léon Bourgeois, which devised a scheme for the use of economic and military sanctions against an aggressor, to be imposed by an international council commanding an international force. Both Britain and the United States were to oppose the French proposal as merely an alliance of the victors to preserve a new balance of power. House revised the Phillimore Plan and then Wilson altered it to include economic as well as military retaliations against transgressor states. He also deleted House's provision for an international court and for a council solely of the great powers, while emphasizing the need for disarmament. This was the plan that Wilson took to Paris for further development.

On arrival in Europe, Wilson had received a copy of the Smuts' proposal for a league. Jan Christian Smuts, one of the Dominion of South Africa's representatives to the peace conference, had outlined a detailed plan for an organization with a general assembly composed of all members and a council comprising the principal powers as permanent members plus several representatives of the lesser states chosen on a rotational basis. A secretariat and a court of arbitration were also included. In essence, Smuts had broadened the British concept to a global organization concerned not merely with deterring aggression but in other ways to promote world progress and peaceful evolution. Wilson was particularly impressed with Smuts' emphasis on the creation of a league as the most important task of the peace conference and his description of the proposed organization as the heir or successor to the disintegrating empires of Europe. The president incorporated a number of ideas from the Smuts plan in his first Paris draft of the Covenant.

Wilson had not required Smuts' encouragement to insist that the League must constitute the heart of the peace treaty. He was determined to combine the charter of the new organization with the territorial and economic settlement; liberal opinion would probably have been disappointed at anything less, and he had long conceived of a league as the vital center of the postwar edifice. He also was to conclude that embodying the League in the peace treaty was the best means of checkmating his opponents in Congress. Perhaps it would have been wiser, as some critics and scholars have suggested, to have incorporated only a general provision for the League in the peace treaty while postponing the details for more leisurely consideration. Although the drafting of the Covenant took place in late afternoon and evening sessions when the main conference was inactive and therefore did not delay the conclusion of the peace treaty, its postponement except for a general reference would have prevented critics from charging that Wilson's obsession with the League had cruelly retarded the restoration of a peace so desperately needed by the world. On the other hand, Wilson feared that if the League were not fully established by the treaty, its creation might be long postponed or avoided altogether by the other great powers. Its existence was needed immediately, he believed, to mitigate some of the inequities which almost inevitably would be incorporated in the general settlement. Finally the historian must note that what was to happen to the Covenant subsequently at the Senate's hands did not indicate that separate negotiations on the League would have led to happier results in that body.

On January 22 President Wilson obtained approval from the Council of Ten of a resolution to make the charter of the League of Nations an integral part of the peace treaty. A special commission was created to draft the document which included the representatives of the great powers and some of the lesser states. A few days later Wilson explained the reasons to a plenary session of the conference: "It is a solemn obligation on our part, therefore, to make permanent arrangements that justice shall be rendered and peace maintained. . . . Settlements may be temporary, but the action of the nations in the interest of peace and justice must be permanent." [13]

---

[13] U. S. State Department, *Papers Relating to the Foreign Relations of the United States: the Paris Peace Conference* (Washington, 1943, 13 vols.), III, 178–181.

The work of writing the League's birth certificate was dominated by Wilson, Smuts, House, and Cecil. Wilson regarded these duties as the most pleasant and rewarding of the conference, and he labored diligently and ably at the task. Lloyd George and Clemenceau, conversely, declined to sit as delegates on the League Commission, preferring to concentrate on political and territorial aspects of the settlement. The commission met in almost daily afternoon or evening sessions and used as its working text a joint Anglo-American draft. France made an effort to incorporate clauses promoting its security against a possible German revival by establishing an international army and general staff under the League. The most that its delegates could obtain, however, was the deletion of a general denunciation of military conscription and the acceptance of a rather innocuous provision for a military advisory committee on possible military sanctions. The major provisions of the Covenant created an assembly of all members for discussion purposes; a council charged with the primary responsibility for preserving peace and deterring aggression, to be composed of the five major powers as permanent members with elected representatives of the smaller states; and a secretariat entrusted with administrative duties. Unanimity was required for council action on substantive matters. Article X of the Covenant embodied Wilson's concept of a mutual guarantee of the territorial integrity and independence of member states as an obligation on all members, and the council was authorized to recommend means to implement the pledge. Sanctions which could be invoked by the council ranged from economic pressure and boycotts of communications to the use of armed force against transgressors. The British Dominions were admitted to the assembly as sovereign states. In general the Anglo-American concept of a more democratic world organization dependent primarily upon public opinion and machinery of conciliation to preserve peace had emerged triumphant over the desires of France for a military grand alliance.

Except for House, who sat with Wilson on the League Commission, the other American commissioners were largely ignored in the drafting of the Covenant. This was probably unfortunate for, apart from the unnecessary humiliation of three able men, their talents could have been used to advantage in the framing of a more tightly written document. Furthermore, some of the objections to the charter held by the three were also current in America and alteration of the League to meet their views might well have enhanced its chances for approval in the Senate.

Lansing had long been sceptical of what he knew of Wilson's thoughts about a collective security organization. He was not an isolationist or even an intense nationalist like Theodore Roosevelt. He did object, however, to a supranational government and wanted to retain American diplomatic freedom. Within that context, he enthusiastically supported codification of international law and the creation of a world court to adjudicate otherwise insoluble issues. Firmly convinced of the inherent peacefulness of democracies, any world organization in his view should restrict membership to democratic states. As he learned more of the plans of Wilson and House, his distress increased. On the trip over on the *George Washington,* he pointed out to the president that the contemplated mutual territorial guarantee, backed by economic and military sanctions, was a dangerous provision if it could be invoked by a simple majority of League members and unworkable if it depended on unanimity. The guaranty, he predicted, would arouse great opposition in the United States: "It is simply loaded with dynamite and he must not go on with it." [14] White and subsequently Bliss concurred that the presidential plan was too vague and contained unwise provisions. Lansing wanted to substitute for the positive mutual guarantee a negative guarantee or a disclaimer by each member that it would do nothing to impair the integrity and independence of other states. He strongly recommended this substitution for Article X as necessary to avoid possible Senate rejection of the Covenant on the grounds of an unconstitutional invasion of the war-making powers of Congress. In addition, the positive guarantee would place the burden of enforcement on the great powers and thereby turn the League into a new alliance, whereas a self-denying ordinance would preserve its universal and equalitarian character.

Despite some gestures of assent, apparently designed to soothe

---

[14] December 11, 1918, Appendix, Lansing Desk Diary.

the irritated secretary of state, House remained committed to the positive guarantee. David Hunter Miller, a law partner of House's son-in-law and one of the experts utilized by Wilson to draft the Covenant, agreed that Lansing's negative guarantee was preferable, especially since it would preclude possible European interventions in Latin America and consequent infringements of the Monroe Doctrine. Wilson apparently never gave the secretary's plan any serious consideration and brushed it aside as a legalistic quibble typical of Lansing's narrow vision. Events were to suggest that it might have been wiser to have adopted a provision similar to Lansing's suggestion. Opposition to the League in the United States was to center on Article X and the mutual guarantee as a dangerous commitment contrary to the Constitution. Not only would a lesser obligation have facilitated Senate approval but it might have improved the image of the League itself in the 1930's. The positive guarantee in practice turned out to be unworkable, or at least it was not successfully utilized. The major defect of Wilson's collective security guarantee proved to be that it depended in fact on great power unanimity to enforce, and yet the significant challenges to world peace could only come from the great powers themselves. A League which promised less initially at least would have had the virtue of being unpretentious and to that extent perhaps would have avoided subsequent disillusionment.

The supreme moment for Wilson at Paris undoubtedly came on February 14 when he presented the hastily drafted Covenant to a plenary session of the conference. After he had read the provisions to the assembled delegates, a note of intensity and hope entered Wilson's speech as he emphasized the importance of the Covenant:

this document . . . is not a straitjacket, but a vehicle of life. A living thing is born . . . it is at one and the same time a practical document and a humane document. . . . I think it is an occasion, therefore, for the most profound satisfaction that this humane decision should have been reached in a matter for which the world has long been waiting. . . .[15]

---

[15] *Foreign Relations, Paris Peace Conference*, III, 209–215.

IV

One of the Fourteen Points had advocated the impartial adjustment of colonial claims with regard to the interests of the inhabitants involved. That principle evolved into the concept of mandates exercised under the jurisdiction of the League of Nations. On the *George Washington*, Wilson had indicated that the most desirable solution for the captured enemy colonies would be to incorporate them into trusteeships held by smaller states and administered for the welfare of the people therein. His idea apparently was derived from the American system for the orderly transition of territories into statehood and from the nation's role of stewardship in the Philippine Islands. Smuts' plan advocated the creation of three classes of mandates under the League to apply to former Russian, Austrian, and Turkish dependencies. Wilson incorporated this proposal into his draft Covenant and enlarged it to include German possessions in Africa and the Pacific area. Liberal sentiment was insistent that the peace should not sanction imperialistic conquests and transfers of dependent people, but Wilson's solution especially ran athwart the aspirations of the British Dominions and Japan.

Lloyd George was willing to accept the mandate system insofar as British claims were involved, but the Dominions of South Africa, Australia, and New Zealand insisted that the German colonies they had seized must be under their control and formally incorporated within their territories. Japan, under the special arrangements with the Allies in 1917, also sought title to the German islands in the Pacific north of the equator. Very sharp exchanges ensued in the Council of Ten between Wilson and Prime Minister William M. Hughes of Australia. Dominion spokesmen justified outright annexation as necessitated by strategic and administrative requirements. Although the debate became sufficiently warm to endanger the continuation of the conference, a compromise was achieved between Wilson's initial idea of small states administering trusteeships and Smuts' exclusion of the German colonies from the proposed mandates. The Turkish territories and the German colonies were to be classified as class A, B, or C mandates and administered under League supervision by the powers which had conquered them. Class A mandates, such as the former Turkish possessions in Asia, by definition required only minimum tutelage prior to achieving complete independence. The German colonies in Southwest Africa and the Pacific islands, allegedly because of sparse and scattered populations or primitive conditions, were classified as C mandates to be administered as integral parts of the mandatary's territory, with military fortifications prohibited. The solution was denounced by many disappointed liberals as hypocrisy, a fraud to conceal an imperialistic division of the spoils. Although Wilson was by no means entirely satisfied, he regarded it as the best solution obtainable. The Allies and Japan were in physical occupation of the areas and could not be pried loose by diplomatic means, but the mandate system at least placed some restrictions on their rule of the colonial peoples and promised eventual self-government for the more advanced. Although it could not then be clearly foreseen, the mandate solution presaged the passing of the age of colonialism. The concept of stewardship under international supervision may not always have worked out well in practice, but morally it implied that exploitation of one people by another was wrong and advocated the ideal goal of independence for all peoples. It must be viewed as in fact a significant if incomplete victory for Wilsonian principles.

V

With the drafting of the Covenant completed, President Wilson left the conference on February 14 for a hurried return to the United States to handle urgent legislative problems. In addition he hoped to explain the Covenant to the people and to dispel the fears and false rumors already voiced by the opposition. When the details of the new charter were published in America, Republican critics had at first hesitated about whether to attack the League as too weak to be of value in preserving world peace or so strong as to diminish American sovereignty and to constitute a world superstate. Apparently it was decided that more political mileage could be found in the second approach and before Wilson could return to the United States, critics had begun the assault. House had urged the president to utilize courtesy and tact by reserving a defense of the Covenant for the congressional foreign relations committees. Instead, after landing to a tumultuous reception in Boston, Senator Lodge's own domain, Wilson made a fighting speech in defense of his handiwork. He challenged the senatorial opposition:

> We set this Nation up to make men free . . . and now we will make men free. If we did not do that all the fame of America would be gone and all her power would be dissipated. She would then have to keep her power for those narrow, selfish, provincial purposes which seem so dear to some minds that have no sweep beyond the nearest horizon. I should welcome no sweeter challenge than that. I have fighting blood in me. . . .[16]

The effort at presidential conciliation of the Senate was obviously reluctant and too belated to have much chance for success. At Wilson's request, the members of the House and Senate foreign affairs committees were his guests at a White House dinner. After the dinner, Wilson spoke for over two hours, attempting to explain and defend the Covenant. Although he maintained a reasonable and persuasive tone, he failed to assuage the hostility of many Republican opponents. Senator Lodge had viewed Wilson's Boston address as a characteristic violation of his own request that public debate on the League be avoided until he could explain it to Congress. Lodge reacted coldly to Wilson's after-dinner defense and recorded afterward that the group had learned nothing really new about the Covenant from the president: "He did not seem to know it very thoroughly and was not able to answer questions." [17] Wilson's supporters left the White House convinced that he had been effective in explaining the charter, while critics were thus unimpressed and unpersuaded. Wilson was highly irritated by the affair and more than ever was disinclined to a conciliatory approach. It would be necessary, he was soon convinced, to

---

[16] *Congressional Record*, 65th Congress, 3rd Session, Vol. 57, 4201–4203.
[17] Henry Cabot Lodge, *The Senate and the League of Nations* (New York: Scribner, 1925), 100.

appeal over the heads of his narrow-minded and partisan opponents directly to the people and to educate them to the great opportunity and the solemn duty awaiting America.

The Republican opposition quickly manifested its hostility. Several speeches critical of the League Covenant were made in the Senate as the session of Congress drew to an end. Lodge spoke two days after the White House dinner and urged that peace be speedily restored by separating the main treaty from the Covenant, which he asserted could then be taken up more leisurely. After warning his audience on the dangers of entangling alliances and the abandonment of isolationism, he indicated in some detail his criticisms of the draft Covenant and recommended that the framers would be wise to give them serious consideration. The Covenant was imprecisely phrased; it must be amended to prevent League intrusion into such domestic questions as immigration restriction; and Article X as it then was phrased endangered the sacred Monroe Doctrine and threatened to involve the United States in wars through the votes of other nations. Other objections or questions were also indicated and Lodge emphasized the need for amendments on these points before the United States should adhere to the League of Nations. The senator concluded his remarks with a slur on the intelligence of some of the framers — clearly intended, it would seem, to infuriate the sensitive president.

Wilson's mood was further darkened when the Republicans compelled the calling of a special session of Congress by using a filibuster to block passage of a needed appropriations bill. The object obviously was to obtain an official platform from which to mount a continuous attack on Wilson's labors at Paris. Finally, as the president prepared to return to Europe, Lodge read to the Senate a pronouncement signed by thirty-nine senators or senators-elect (six more than would be needed to prevent the necessary two-thirds majority to approve the treaty), that the Covenant as presently drafted was unacceptable. This Republican "Round-Robin" not only gave Wilson notice of the existence of a determined opposition but clearly informed his Paris conferees that the president probably would not be able to control the new Congress. His diplomatic position was weakened and his subsequent labors at Paris for a reasonable settlement were greatly compounded. Unfortunately, although understandably, Wilson retaliated by telling an audience in New York City that regardless of the amazing ignorance and selfish vision of some American critics, when the completed treaty was laid before the Senate the Covenant would be so tied to the general settlement as to defy separation without detroying the whole.

Despite his defiant reaction in America, Wilson at Paris reluctantly reconvened the League of Nations Commission. He feared that appeasing the Senate would only encourage his opponents at home and that other countries would exploit reopening the subject to force the incorporation of enfeebling changes of their own. On the other hand, friends of the League, such as former-President Taft, strongly recommended certain amendments as necessary to prevent serious opposition to the Covenant. In several exhausting evening sessions of the committee, Wilson and House secured adoption of the desired amendments and fended off efforts of other powers to include further alterations. Provisions that a member could decline a proffered mandate and the exemption from League jurisdiction of questions affecting the domestic affairs of a state met little opposition. Greater difficulty was experienced with the proposals that the Monroe Doctrine should be specifically safeguarded from League control or abrogation and that a member could renounce membership in the League after two years notification and the faithful performance of all obligations.

Great Britain and France objected that these changes would seriously impair the ability of the League to preserve peace and to guarantee the security of its members. Lloyd George declined to approve a clause recognizing the Monroe Doctrine with the reasonable argument that it was an improper recognition of a purely regional arrangement. The actual motive behind the British objection, however, was to bargain with the concession in order to persuade the United States to curtail its naval construction. Wartime programs if completed would create an American navy at least equal to the British fleet or would compel a costly naval construction race by England to retain its traditional supremacy. Committed to a policy of security through naval superiority and unable to perceive any practical American need for parity, Lloyd George was determined to obtain an agreement supporting the naval status quo. It seems that he also still feared that Wilson would launch a vigorous effort in behalf of freedom of the seas. Americans, however, recalled only too well the numerous Allied violations of neutral rights in the early years of the war, and some citizens also were convinced that naval equality was required because of potential danger from the Anglo-Japanese alliance. President Wilson had directed continuation of naval expansion even after the Armistice, apparently in part to strengthen his diplomatic position at the peace conference. The French motive in raising objections to the proposed amendments allegedly weakening the security of France, seems to have been to try to obtain additional safeguards against Germany. Compromises were finally arranged and the amendments were approved. The United States agreed to suspend naval construction planned beyond the existing program and to consult with Great Britain regularly on naval problems; France, the evidence suggests, was mollified by the provisions for military occupation of the Rhineland area. The League Commission then completed its work and the revised Covenant was approved by the plenary session of the Peace Conference on April 28.

President Wilson was unwilling to go beyond these changes in the Covenant to assuage critics in America. He viewed the subject as closed thereafter; the Senate would have to accept the Covenant as it was or do the unbelievable and reject it. Later during the conference, when Lansing relayed additional criticism from America and suggestions for changes relating to Article X, Wilson replied that it was too late and that the only answer to trouble makers in the United States was to meet them in a direct counterattack. The Senate could either accept the existing Covenant or reject the entire treaty, and he promised to adopt a militant and aggressive course upon his return to America. His attitude augered ill for the conciliation and compromise necessary to secure senatorial approval of the treaty.

CHAPTER VIII

The Russian Problem
and the Peace Conference

THE SPECTER of Bolshevik Russia loomed in the background of the proceedings at the Paris Peace Conference. A quick peace was necessary, it was universally agreed, to halt the spread of its subversive ideology. How to cope with the regime in Russia, however, remained an unresolved problem and in a real sense was the major failure of the peace conference.

I

The March Revolution in Russia coincided with America's own transition into belligerency. As President Wilson revealed in his war address, it was easier to rationalize the war entry on ideological grounds after a provisional republic had supplanted the czarist autocracy. Unfortunately, neither the American people nor their government had much knowledge or understanding of the Russian situation. It was too readily assumed that Russia would rapidly become a stable constitutional democracy; the war weariness of Russia's masses and the pervasiveness of revolutionary ideology were inadequately comprehended. Apart from the factors of remoteness and traditional disinterest in eastern Europe, the lack of adequate information about Russia during the war years could be largely attributed to the weaknesses and confusion of American representation in that vast and turbulent land. Ambassador David R. Francis, a Missouri politician, lacked diplomatic experience and knowledge of the Russian language and history. Probably he should have been replaced. His task was rendered more difficult by the profusion of amateur diplomats resulting from the several special war missions the United States established in Russia. Edgar Sisson and Arthur Bullard of the Committee on Public Information, William Boyce Thompson and Raymond Robins of the American Red Cross, together with the military *attaché*, were all involved to a confusing degree in dealing with the various Russian factions and recommending policy to the Washington authorities.

Soon after the declaration of war, Lansing and other advisers recommended to the president that a special mission be sent to Russia to investigate conditions including rumors that Russia might withdraw from the war, and to promote the common war effort. President Wilson concurred and Elihu Root was selected for the task. It was revelatory of the comparative ignorance of Russian conditions by the American government that a well-known conservative such as Root should have been designated to head a mission to an increasingly socialist state. Aloof and unbending, Root apparently was incapable of any great sympathy for Russia and its problems. He reportedly remarked on his tour that although he was a lover of democracy, he could not tolerate filth and disorder. It was inevitable that his mission aroused much criticism and hostility among the Russian socialists and radicals.

After exhausting rounds of official receptions and platitudinous speeches, the Root mission returned to America in August 1917 with an amazingly optimistic report. Aid should be promised to the provisional government, contingent upon Russia's continuation in the war against the Central powers. Perhaps, as the diplomat and historian George F. Kennan has suggested, a more understanding attitude on the part of the United States and the Allies, recognizing the near exhaustion of the Russian people caused by the war, would have aided the provisional regime in its efforts at survival. Root did recommend a propaganda campaign to counter pacifist and radical opposition in Russia to the continuation of the war and the utilization of recreational experts from the Young Men's Christian Association to bolster sagging Russian army morale.

In the light of recent Russian army reverses, mutiny and desertions, and an abortive Bolshevik coup, the Root report was lamentably inadequate and unrealistic. Even Secretary Lansing, admittedly with a sketchy knowledge of Russian conditions, marveled at the optimism of Root and his colleagues. Lansing was personally convinced that the Russian Revolution would undergo an evolution similar to the bloody French Revolution, from moderation to a reign of terror and finally reaction and military dictatorship. Yet he felt there was no choice but to accept Root's suggestions and to make every effort to bolster the provisional government: "If Mr. Root is wrong, nothing that we can do will stay the current which is toward a period of disorder and national impotency. All our efforts will amount to nothing; they will simply be chips swept along by the tide to be swallowed up in the calamity which seems to me in store for Russia." [1]

Lansing's gloomy forecast proved to be only too accurate. Aid was extended to the provisional government to the extent of $325 millions, and Red Cross representatives, Y.M.C.A. recreational aides, propagandists, and railway experts arrived to try to strengthen Russia's participation in the great crusade against German autocracy. But as Lansing had feared, all proved to be of little avail. The liberal ministry of Premier Prince George Lvov gave way to the moderate socialist one of Alexander Kerensky. Kerensky was no more successful in promoting military efficiency or coping with growing popular desires for peace and the mounting radical assaults on the government. On November 7, 1917, Nikolai Lenin engineered a successful Bolshevik overthrow of the Kerensky regime. Within a few weeks, the new government called for an immediate peace without conquests and indemnities, denounced the United States and the Allies as waging an imperialistic war, and published many of the Allied secret treaties and understandings. An armistice was concluded with Germany that removed Russia from the war and enabled the Central powers to concentrate manpower on the western front for an attempt at a decisive victory in

---

[1] "Memorandum on the Russian Situation and the Root Mission," August 9, 1917, Confidential Memoranda, Robert Lansing Papers.

France. President Wilson's implied appeal, in the Fourteen Points address, to the Russian people to remain in the great struggle for democracy revealed once more both his lack of knowledge about Russia and his idealistic faith that the Russian people were inherently democratic. They failed to heed Wilson — on March 3 the Bolshevik representatives signed a peace treaty at Brest-Litovsk with the Central powers.

II

The initial American reaction to the Bolshevik seizure focused on its military implications. The Communist regime could not be recognized because it was dedicated to peace at any price with the Central powers; furthermore, no one in authority believed that the handful of doctrinaire and impractical Communist radicals could long retain their tenuous hold on power. In addition to military considerations, President Wilson retained his rather misplaced faith in the innate idealism and democratic tendencies of the Russian masses. He disliked the Bolshevik regime as an undemocratic conspiracy that had destroyed the democratic and constitutional promise of the provisional government. The anticapitalist aspects of Communism apparently were not taken very seriously by the president, who instead saw the real issue everywhere as one of democracy versus autocracy. Colonel House shared much of Wilson's evaluation and recommended that Russia should not be branded as an enemy but that every occasion should be utilized to encourage and support Russian democratic movements.

Secretary Lansing was almost alone among high Washington officials in giving close and serious study to Communist ideology. He concluded that the new regime could not be recognized not only because its future was highly doubtful but because of its ambitions and doctrines. Early in December 1917, after the Bolshevik armistice with the Central powers, the secretary advised Wilson that a public statement should be released announcing that the purposes and character of Lenin's government precluded diplomatic recognition. It was an undemocratic regime which had seized power by violence and apparently did not represent the true sentiments of the Russian people (the popularly elected Constituent Assembly, in which the Bolsheviks were a decided minority, subsequently was suppressed by Lenin). As a nation dedicated to the growth of democracy, the United States could no more condone a dictatorship of the working class than it could an autocracy of birth and wealth. In a subsequent memorandum, Lansing noted the confusion of observers about Russian conditions, which he shared: "The Russian situation is to me an unanswered and unanswerable riddle." [2] But even if the Bolsheviks should by some miracle retain power, the regime could not be recognized since it proclaimed class warfare and the overthrow of all existing governments, the dictatorship of the Communist Party, and the destruction of private property and the principles of nationality. In confident tones, similar to the later views of his nephew, John Foster Dulles, Lansing predicted that Communism contained within it the seeds of its own inevitable destruction. Contrary to the conviction widely prevalent in America and Europe, however, he did not believe that Lenin and his chief aide, Leon Trotsky, were merely paid German agents sent to Russia to destroy its military power. Despite their war on civilization and their efforts to elevate the "ignorant and incapable mass of humanity" to power, they probably were "honest in purpose and utterly dishonest in methods." [3] Lansing's analysis was one of the earliest and most astute among the leaders within the Allied camp.

Although President Wilson declined at the time to issue a public statement, he did concur that nonrecognition was the only wise policy. As did Lansing, he apparently viewed that approach as a temporary course, a do-nothing policy while awaiting the inevitable Bolshevik collapse and the emergence of new forces. Unlike the secretary, however, who forecast a bloody reign of terror followed by a military dictatorship, Wilson retained his belief in Russia's democratic future. Lansing stated to the press that Lenin's regime would not be recognized, and

---

[2] "Memorandum on the Russian Situation," December 7, 1917, Confidential Memoranda, Lansing Papers.

[3] *Ibid.*

the ambassador of the defunct provisional government continued to be accorded official status by the State Department. In Russia, American diplomats by mid-1918 had been ordered to cease limited and even informal contacts with the Soviet government and to withdraw from Bolshevik-held areas. Nonrecognition was thus adopted in 1917 and by the end of 1918 had become a fixed policy toward the Communist regime. Whatever the validity of subsequent criticisms of nonrecognition when it was continued into the 1920's and early 1930's, it was a defensible course in 1917–1919. Apart from idealistic and moral considerations, it was dictated by several very practical factors. The Bolshevik hold on power was tenuous, and military necessity seemed to require some kind of Allied counteraction in Russia. Unfortunately, nonrecognition in itself was not a substitute for a constructive policy and neither the United States nor the Allies was able to develop a more promising approach.

In the Fourteen Points address in January 1918, President Wilson proclaimed two additional aspects of America's policy toward the Russian Revolution: nonintervention and, by implication, the maintenance of Russia's territorial integrity. The United States was a disinterested friend, he asserted, which only sought an opportunity for the Russian people to achieve freedom and peace. The test of the good intentions of other countries, Wilson proclaimed, would be revealed in the subsequent treatment accorded Russia, and he urged the evacuation of the territories occupied by the enemy and noninterference by all while the Russian people determined for themselves the form of government under which they would live. Throughout the remainder of his administration the president and Secretary Lansing opposed efforts to dismember the Russian empire and were unwilling to recognize or encourage the several separatist movements which flowered after the Bolshevik coup. Although the Allied governments were tempted to back various anti-Bolshevik and nationalist activities, the United States was saved from that type of involvement by its hesitations on moral and practical grounds. In addition to their views on Russia's integrity, Wilson and Lansing were anxious not to drive the Bolsheviks into closer ties with Germany. Some efforts were made to encourage the "white" forces of General Alexei Kaledin

in the Don region and Admiral Alexander Kolchak in Siberia —
Lansing urged Wilson to "play with all of them" [4] to promote
the emergence of a pro-western government in Russia — but
these proved to be abortive or half-hearted moves.

III

Repeated Allied requests and military exigencies did eventually
result in American consent to limited armed interventions in
Russia. Almost as soon as the Bolsheviks had seized control,
London and Paris began to bombard Washington with urgent
pleas for intervention. First the French government and then the
British made formal overtures for large-scale action designed to
halt German advances in the east and to return Russia to the war
as an active partner. Although the American government declined to endorse action, which in its view was not militarily
imperative, the proposals continued. The Allied countries were
near exhaustion and hard pressed on the western front. When
a great German offensive began on March 21, they became
almost hysterical in their pleas for armed intervention to restore
a front in Russia and to halt the movement of German troops
from the eastern front to France. The Japanese government,
although still under the control of moderates interested in cooperation with the United States, also favored intervention.
Important elements in Japan hoped to exploit the Russian Revolution to expand Japanese interests in Manchuria and perhaps
in maritime Siberia. A security motive was also involved. Japanese officials feared that a German-dominated Russia or a
Bolshevik-controlled one would endanger Japan's special interests in China and perhaps the security of the Japanese home
islands as well. The faction within the government which favored
large-scale action in Siberia regardless of American wishes,
however, was at least nominally checked by the more moderate
group which placed a higher value on good relations with the
United States and declined to sanction intervention except in
cooperation with President Wilson.

---

[4] Lansing Memorandum, January 29, 1918, State Department File 861.00/
1048 1/2, National Archives.

Chaotic conditions within Russia — a scene of frenzied civil war between Bolsheviks, anti-Bolsheviks, and separatists — increased Allied anxiety. It was feared, or at least argued as an excuse for action, that the vast war supplies shipped from America and western Europe and accumulated at Murmansk in northern Russia and Vladivostok in Siberia would fall into the hands of the advancing German armies. Alarming if unsubstantiated stories circulated that the Bolshevik authorities, allegedly German agents, were freeing and arming large numbers of German and Austrian prisoners of war. Intervention at Murmansk and at Vladivostok would, it was claimed, save the supplies, halt the German advances, and restore the eastern front by reestablishing a pro-Allied government in Russia. Finally, the plight of the Czechoslovak legion contributed additional military and emotional arguments for intervention. These troops, over 45,000 strong, had been fighting on Russian soil against the Central Powers and now wanted to withdraw via Vladivostok to France and the western front. While the Czechs were dispersed along the Trans-Siberian railway, clashes occurred with local Bolshevik soviets and full-fledged fighting ensued. Allied proposals for intervention subsequently emphasized the need to rescue the brave Czechs and to protect their escape port at Vladivostok. The demand for aid to the Czechs was echoed by large segments of the American press and public. Wilson finally capitulated, in June and July, and in separate decisions accepted limited military operations in northern Russia and at Vladivostok.

The motives for American intervention in Siberia, which was a larger action than that in north Russia, have been warmly debated by scholars. A few have attributed the decision to anti-Bolshevik purposes, the desire to topple Lenin's regime and establish a capitalistic and pro-western government in its place. The generally accepted view has explained Wilson's obviously reluctant approval of intervention as designed to avert unilateral Japanese action in Siberia and thereby to protect Russia's integrity and the Open Door Policy in the Far East. The latest studies emphasize that the decision can be understood only within the context of the war raging in Europe. Military imperatives seemed to demand intervention: the great German

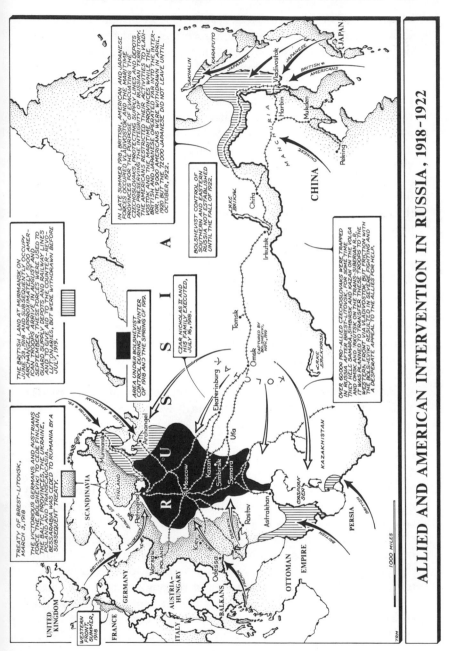

ALLIED AND AMERICAN INTERVENTION IN RUSSIA, 1918–1922

TREATY OF BREST-LITOVSK, MARCH 3, 1918

THE VICTORIOUS GERMANS AND AUSTRIANS FORCE THE BOLSHEVIKI TO CEDE FINLAND, THE BALTIC STATES, THE UKRAINE, POLAND AND TRANSCAUCASIA. BESSARABIA WAS CEDED TO RUMANIA BY A SUBSEQUENT TREATY.

THE BRITISH LAND AT MURMANSK ON JUNE 23, 1918 AND SUBSEQUENTLY OCCUPY ARCHANGEL. APPROXIMATELY 5,000 AMER-ICAN TROOPS ARRIVE IN AUGUST AND SEPTEMBER. THESE FORCES WERE USED TO GUARD SUPPLY DEPOTS AND RAILWAY LINES AND TO GIVE AID TO THE COUNTER-REVO-LUTIONARIES, BUT WERE WITHDRAWN BEFORE JULY, 1919.

IN LATE SUMMER 1918, BRITISH, AMERICAN AND JAPANESE FORCES OCCUPIED VLADIVOSTOK AND THE MARITIME PROVINCES FOR THE PURPOSE OF EVACUATING THE CZECHOSLOVAKS, PROTECTING SUPPLY DEPOTS AND PRESERVING THE TERRITORIAL INTEGRITY OF RUSSIA. THE AMERICANS RESTRICTED THEIR ACTIVITIES TO VLADI-VOSTOK AND THE MARITIME PROVINCES, WHILE THE BRITISH AND JAPANESE OPERATED OVER A WIDER TERRI-TORY. THE 9,000 AMERICANS WERE WITHDRAWN IN APRIL, 1920, BUT THE 72,000 JAPANESE DID NOT LEAVE UNTIL OCTOBER, 1922.

AREA UNDER BOLSHEVIST CONTROL DURING THE WINTER OF 1918 AND THE SPRING OF 1919.

CZAR NICHOLAS II AND HIS FAMILY EXECUTED, JULY 16, 1918.

BOLSHEVIST CONTROL OF SOUTHERN AND EASTERN RUSSIA NOT ESTABLISHED UNTIL THE FALL OF 1922.

OVER 60,000 PRO-ALLIED CZECHOSLOVAKS WERE TRAPPED IN RUSSIA AFTER BREST-LITOVSK. FOR SOME TIME THEY HELD SAMARA, SIMBIRSK AND KAZAN ON THE VOLGA AND OMSK AND IRKUTSK ON THE TRANS-SIBERIAN R.R. IT WAS PLANNED TO TRANSFER THESE TROOPS TO THE WESTERN FRONT VIA VLADIVOSTOK, BUT FRICTION WITH THE BOLSHEVIKI RESULTED IN SEVERE FIGHTING AND A DESPERATE APPEAL TO THE ALLIES FOR HELP.

WESTERN FRONT, SUMMER, 1918

UNITED KINGDOM

FRANCE

ITALY

GERMANY

AUSTRIA–HUNGARY

BALKANS

OTTOMAN EMPIRE

SCANDINAVIA

FINLAND

Petrograd

Murmansk

Archangel

Moscow

Kazan

Simbirsk

Samara

Ufa

Ekaterinburg

Omsk

Tomsk

Irkutsk

Rostov

Odessa

Warsaw

Astrakhan

R U S S I A

CZAR NICHOLAS II

CASPIAN SEA

PERSIA

KAZAKHSTAN

OTTOMAN EMPIRE

CHINA

MANCHURIA

Peking

Mukden

Harbin

China

Vladivostok

SAKHALIN

KARAFUTO

JAPAN

JAPANESE

BRITISH + AMERICANS

CHINESE

CZECHOSLOVAKS CAPTURED BY BOLSHEVIKI, NOV., 1919

1000 MILES

TRM

offensive on the western front, fears of deep German penetration in Russia, and the plight of the Czech legion. The memoirs and documents of the period suggest that all of these considerations were involved to some degree.

Japanese unilateral intervention was feared in Washington primarily because of its probable effects on the Russian people rather than a current apprehension of Japanese territorial expansion. Colonel House, who for a long time had objected to military intervention, repeatedly argued that Japanese action alone, as urged by the Allies and Japan, would arouse racial and historic antagonisms in Russia and would tend to force the Bolsheviks to depend on German support. He found the enthusiasm of the British and French for Japanese military operations difficult to comprehend and he feared that the effects would lower the moral position of the Allies and perhaps weaken popular support for the war in America. He was not opposed to Japan's legitimate interests, however, as he made clear in a letter to British Foreign Secretary Balfour. He had no desire, he assured Balfour, to challenge Japan's position in Far Eastern affairs. House also emphasized that point to the president, to whom he wrote that Japan would have to be reckoned with if its citizens were not permitted to help exploit underdeveloped areas in Siberia and Manchuria.

Lansing shared these views. For that reason he early made a distinction between Siberia and north Russia, for in the latter no racial issue would be aroused by the landing of American, British, and French troops. Lansing recorded in his private memoranda the conviction that if Japan alone intervened in Siberia, the effects would be disastrous in terms of Russian hostility and pro-German reactions. He could envision little military advantage from intervention and agreed with the American military advisers that chaotic conditions and logistics precluded reestablishment of an eastern front against Germany. As for the 600,000 tons of supplies at Vladivostok, he concluded that they could hardly be speedily moved to Germany over thousands of miles of railroad and through turbulent areas. Yet he recognized and sympathized with Japan's fears of the spread of Communism and its desire to construct a *cordon sanitaire* to contain the virus in the Far East. In May 1918, he discussed "Bolshevism and its dangers to all gov[ernmen]ts, especially Japan" with the Japanese ambassador.[5] Even later after many tensions with Japan over the purposes and conduct of the intervention, the secretary recognized the peril of Communist Russia to Japan and expressed confidence that the Japanese government did not plan the annexation of Siberian territory: "we ought not to raise any objection to Japan sending a sufficient force to check the Bolshevik advance [,] for the spread of Bolshevism in the Far East would be a dreadful menace to civilization."[6]

President Wilson on at least one occasion did speak of the possible need of American participation in order to restrain Japan, but his discussions with House and Lansing indicated that he too was primarily concerned about the adverse effects of unilateral Japanese action upon the Russian people and factions. He did not want to stir up racial hatred or to provide the Bolsheviks with a nationalistic banner to increase their appeal in Russia. It seems clear that he, like House and Lansing, would have preferred to have confined American efforts at bolstering Russia to a large-scale economic aid and relief program. When armed action finally seemed imperative to him, it apparently was not in order to restrain Japanese expansion, whatever his later fears on that point.

The immediate and overriding reasons for American participation in the interventions were military. On July 2, 1918, the Allied Supreme War Council recommended the landing of large forces in Siberia to save Russia from German domination and to rescue the Czechoslovaks. Wilson finally agreed that action was necessary. German advances in north Russia had to be checked and the supplies at Murmansk and Archangel protected; and in the Far East sympathy and military necessity required the rescue of the Czechoslovak legion and the disarming of German and Austrian prisoners of war. At a White House conference on July 6, President Wilson reached a final decision for intervention at Vladivostok as a small-scale Japa-

---

[5] May 24, 1918, Lansing Desk Diary.
[6] "Advisability of Withdrawing Our Troops from Siberia," November 30, 1919, Confidential Memoranda, Lansing Papers.

nese-American venture to aid the Czechs against the German danger. He was determined, however, that there was to be no interference in the internal affairs and politics of Russia nor any threat to Russia's territorial integrity.

Yet an anti-Bolshevik motive was involved. In June a note to Lansing argued, "if a stable form of government, such as would appeal primarily to the Russian people who are opposed to the German influence in Russia, could be established through military intervention, in Asiatic Russia . . . the moral effect upon the balance of Russia would be incalculable." [7] The Wilson-drafted *aide-memoire* of July 17 to the Allied representatives, after disavowing intervention for political — that is, anti-Bolshevik — purposes, explained the landing of military forces at Vladivostok as designed to support the Czechs and to stabilize any resultant Russian efforts at self-government and self-defense. Earlier, in discussion of the probable effects of the Siberian venture with the Japanese ambassador, Lansing had noted the possibility that the Czechoslovak troops could be used as a nucleus for the formation of a popular and pro-Ally Russian government. Wilson himself referred to their use to organize resistance against Germany as "the shadow of a plan that might be worked, with Japanese and other assistance. These people [Czechoslovaks] are the cousins of the Russians." [8] It seems probable, therefore, that a secondary motive behind American intervention was the hope of Wilson and his advisers that the mere presence of Allied troops would encourage the formation of a popular democratic government and the overthrow of the Bolshevik regime. In that limited sense, intervention was covertly and passively anti-Bolshevik in purpose.

American involvement in the interventions had a quixotic and unrealistic character. President Wilson continued to oppose efforts to restore an eastern front as unwise on moral and practical grounds, yet he had agreed to limited armed action to rescue the stranded Czechoslovaks and to "steady" non-

---

[7] Unsigned Memorandum, Indexed as from Lansing's Office, June 17, 1918, State Department File 861.00/2146 1/2, Archives. [Author unknown.]
[8] Wilson to Lansing June 17, 1918, *Foreign Relations, Lansing Papers*, II, 363.

Bolshevik efforts at self-government. At the same time he wanted the intervening powers to avoid direct interferences in Russia's internal politics, and he so instructed the American military commanders involved. The Czechoslovak legion even then was engaged in open fighting with the Bolsheviks and, far from hurrying to escape Russia through Vladivostok, was supporting various "white" movements against the Communists. In north Russia the United States was quickly disturbed at clear indications that the Allied commanders were pursuing political goals and hoped to reconstruct a Russian war front running from Archangel to the areas held by the anti-Bolsheviks around Omsk in Siberia. Japan in the Far East brought in far more troops than the American government believed necessary, until its forces numbered over 70,000 men to the approximately 9000 under the command of the American general. Difficulties multiplied, for while the American commander, General William S. Graves, carefully adhered to his orders to avoid political involvement and to confine operations to the guarding of supplies and the railway lines essential to evacuation of the Czechoslovaks, the Allies openly supported anti-Bolshevik movements. Japan particularly appeared determined to acquire control over the former Russian sphere of influence in central and northern Manchuria and to support anti-Bolshevik puppets in the Amur Basin and the maritime provinces of Siberia. The consequence was an American decision, prior to the Armistice, to dissociate itself from the Allies. The futility of the Allied military efforts at recreation of the eastern front was pointed out to them in a memorandum in September 1918, and Wilson declined to sanction those efforts by reinforcing the American contingents.

IV

The conclusion of the armistice with Germany in November 1918 removed the military justification behind the interventions. President Wilson was convinced that Communism reflected Russian economic and social distress and that on both moral and practical grounds military intervention was an inadequate antidote. He was not opposed to socialistic governments per se, as long as they were democratic in nature. As he wrote Lansing, in an oversimplified analysis: "The real thing with which to stop Bolshevism is food." [9] At the Paris Peace Conference, therefore, he joined Prime Minister Lloyd George in opposition to schemes for direct military action against the Bolshevik government. Lloyd George concurred that Communism indicated grave underlying social ills in Russia and that in any case the principles of self-determination precluded further intervention. Clemenceau, however, still hoped to strangle Bolshevism by economic blockade and he was attracted by the proposals of Winston Churchill, the British minister of war, for the sending of volunteer troops and large quantities of military supplies to support the anti-Bolshevik forces. Lloyd George and Wilson vetoed such plans and the American president made it clear to the Council of Ten that in his view the Allied forces already in Russia had achieved nothing positive and should be withdrawn as quickly as possible. Further action would harm the Russian people, outrage public sentiment in America and Great Britain, and strengthen the hold of the Bolsheviks within Russia.

An effort was made to end the civil war by inviting representatives of all Russian factions to a conference planned for Prinkipo Island in the Sea of Marmara. The Bolsheviks signified acceptance but the White groups refused to attend with the Communists and the plan was stillborn. An unofficial fact-finding mission to Moscow by William C. Bullitt, a young and idealistic member of the American delegation, also failed despite his report that the Bolsheviks were firmly in control and were willing to accept an armistice as the prelude to peace negotiations among the factions and to the withdrawal of Allied troops. Apparently because when he made his report prospects seemed unusually promising for a sweeping victory by Admiral Kolchak's armies, driving westward from Omsk, Bullitt's proposal with its promise of peace and probable diplomatic recognition of the Bolsheviks received no official attention. Perhaps also Wilson decided that the pledges of

---

[9] Wilson to Lansing, January 10, 1919, Wilson Papers.

Lenin and Trotsky were totally unreliable. Public opinion in America and England in any event was adverse to recognition of the Communist regime. The Council of Four, therefore, agreed to promise Kolchak further aid and support, though not yet diplomatic recognition, in return for assurances about eventual free elections, social reforms, and democratic government in Russia. Wilson reluctantly agreed, although he told his colleagues that he had long thought it desirable to withdraw and to let the Russians fight to a decision themselves on the future of their country. Kolchak proved to be incapable of surviving without the transfusion of additional Allied manpower; by June 1919 his drive on Moscow had collapsed and by the end of the year his capital at Omsk had fallen to Trotsky's Red armies. Shortly thereafter his regime completely disintegrated. To avoid direct clashes with the Bolshevik forces, and because of dissatisfaction with Japan's course in Siberia, American troops were therefore withdrawn from Vladivostok by April 1920. The units in north Russia had been removed earlier, in June 1919.

The fruits of the limited interventions were bitter. The Bolshevik government accused the United States of hostility and a deliberate effort, along with the Allies, to strangle Communism in its cradle. There seems little doubt but that the effects of the interventions were to worsen the Russian civil war and paradoxically at the same time to increase the popular appeal and strength of the Bolshevik party and regime. Within America many liberals came to deplore the interventions and to attribute subsequent Communist noncooperative actions and attitudes of enmity and suspicion primarily to that cause.

In recent years some scholars have ceased castigating the intervention as unwise in itself and have begun to criticize Wilson for not acting decisively enough. More extensive aid to the anti-Bolshevik regimes, it has been argued, perhaps would have toppled the Communists, while support of the separatist movements would have circumscribed Soviet power. Yet a more extensive American involvement would not have been assured of success. A genuine revolution was underway in Russia which was beyond the power of the United States and the Allies to suppress. Efforts to do so would merely have led to even more turmoil and chaos in Russia and to increased bitterness in subsequent relations with the Communist state.

Wilson undoubtedly was too visionary in his faith that the Russian people if left alone would find their way toward a democratic form of society and government, and his acquiescence in limited interventions in northern Russia and Siberia was, in view of Allied purposes and Russian conditions, highly impractical and unworkable. Yet he avoided full-scale military intervention, with all its probable consequences, and thereby saved both Russia and the West from an even costlier entanglement. He clung tenaciously to his belief that principle and reason required nonintervention in the Russian Revolution. In picking his path through a jungle of conflicting pressures and interests, he displayed much wisdom and commendable restraint. A half-century later, it is hard to perceive how he could have achieved more.

CHAPTER IX

The Struggle for an Enduring Peace

U PON PRESIDENT WILSON'S return to the peace conference, on
March 14, he immediately revealed discontent with House's
management of affairs during his absence. From the first days
of the conference there had been much discussion of the need
to conclude a preliminary treaty embodying the essential military
and naval terms. With the lifting of wartime restrictions and
the return to at least a semblance of peace, it was hoped that
the conference could approach the framing of the definitive
peace treaty at a more leisurely pace. Wilson approved of the
idea of peace in two installments, but evidently he insisted that
the Covenant of the League must be incorporated in the first
treaty. Apparently he conceived of the preliminary convention
as an executive agreement or a kind of exalted armistice, rather
than a formal treaty, which would allow him to bypass the
American Senate and get the League of Nations into immediate
operation; then when the definitive treaty came before the
Senate, that body would presumably find it more difficult to
change or reject a functioning League in which the United
States was already a participant. During his absence, however,
the Allied leaders persuaded House to accept the inclusion of
non-military terms in the projected preliminary arrangement.
The French government feared that if the territorial and economic provisions were separated from the military terms and
were imposed later, Germany might be encouraged to resist.
It would be safer, Clemenceau and his advisers believed, to
present all the basic terms at the same time and while the Allied
armies were still at full strength. The enlarged project obviously could be put into effect only if it were submitted to the
Senate as a treaty, and so Wilson, greatly irritated at House's

compromising, decided to abandon the scheme. The subsequent cooling of Wilson's relations with Colonel House probably had its beginning in the president's keen disappointment at this development.

I

The overriding problem complicating almost every phase of peace making with Germany was the determination of France to obtain lasting security against a revival of German power. As a consequence, the major clauses were interlocking compromises which tried to achieve a workable balance between security requirements and the dictates of justice. When discussions began on the military clauses, France proposed a German army to be composed of a maximum of 200,000 men conscripted for one year of service. French officials were unwilling to have conscription prohibited, in apprehension that the ban might be made universal in application and thus affect the French conscript system; if Germany were limited to a small and short-term conscripted army, it was believed that no high levels of military efficiency and skills could be attained. The Anglo-Americans, who would have preferred a general abolition of conscription, advocated instead a German army of 200,000 men who would voluntarily enlist for minimum terms of twelve years each. Clemenceau reluctantly accepted the plan but insisted that the number be reduced to a maximum of 100,000 men, as the longer term of service would otherwise permit Germany to build a large trained cadre of commissioned and non-commissioned officers able to lead the nation-in-arms whenever opportune. Most of these provisions had been tentatively hammered out during Wilson's trip to America. Upon his return he accepted them with reluctance, though with minor modifications. The clauses embodied in the Treaty set a limitation of 100,000 men for the German army and prohibited use of tanks, poison gas, and military aircraft; and the general staff, the central planning agency, was to be disbanded. The navy was also to be severely restricted in manpower and the number and tonnage of surface warships sharply curtailed; possession of submarines was entirely prohibited. These terms were theoretically related to the provisions of the Covenant for universal arms reduction to the level consistent with internal security. Wilson hoped that German disarmament would in fact serve as the vestibule to that goal. Subsequent events were to disappoint that hope and an embittered Germany alone was to remain partially disarmed.

The French government made a major effort to dismember Germany and to establish the Rhineland area as an antonomous state under the control of France. A similar desire was expressed for annexation of the Saar Valley. With the return to France of Alsace and Lorraine, Germany thereby would be deprived of a very large slice of territory and the French frontier in effect solidly based on the Rhine River. These proposals were defended on the grounds of defense against possible future German invasions, France's historic frontiers before 1814, and the need for compensation for war damages. Detachment of the Rhineland would deprive Germany of nearly six million people and extensive industry, and loss of the Saar would strip Germany of a number of factories and coal mines. Wilson opposed both of these demands as contrary to the principle of self-determination, an affront to German nationalism which would disturb the peace of Europe indefinitely if consummated. He was also cognizant of the serious economic consequences for Germany and for all Europe. Finally, he did not desire the permanent elimination of German power and influence. Lloyd George joined him in opposition to the French schemes, out of principle and practical considerations forbade what they reissue would be created threatening the future peace of Europe. On these issues, the British and American leaders stood firm; principle and practical considerations forbade what they regarded as unrealistic and excessive French desires for security and revenge.

Clemenceau fought vigorously for the Rhineland and the Saar. At one conference the French premier angrily accused Wilson of being pro-German; when the president replied that it seemed that Clemenceau wanted him to leave the conference and return home, the furious premier retorted no, but that he himself would and he stalked from the room. Lloyd George finally suggested a compromise proposal that the Rhineland be demilitarized and left within the German republic, with French security to be pledged by Great Britain and the United States. As for the Saar, all admitted that France was entitled to compensation for the coal mines in northern France which had been flooded by the retreating German armies. Wilson, however, remained adamant against annexation. Lloyd George concurred, but under pressure he shifted to a position establishing the Saar as an autonomous area, presumably under French control.

In early April the deadlock reached dangerous proportions. All the unresolved issues seemed to reach the crisis stage simultaneously. In the League Commission, Britain and France were resisting the proposed changes in the Covenant recognizing the Monroe Doctrine and the right to withdraw from membership; the reparations question was the center of sharp disagreement between the Americans and the Allies; and the French were adamant in their demands for security through detachment of the Rhineland and the Saar Valley. On April 3 Wilson suddenly became violently ill. His temperature rose alarmingly and he was wracked with spasms of coughing and labored breathing. His doctor diagnosed it as influenza, but medical experts now believe that the president was the victim of arteriosclerosis, worsened by the tensions and conflicts at Paris, and that he possibly had suffered a mild cerebral thrombosis or stroke. For three days he lay ill in bed; as he began to recover, the other members of the Big Four met in the adjoining room, with House sitting in as Wilson's representative. Grimly the sick president vetoed proposal after proposal which he felt fell far short of an equitable solution to the Saar and the Rhineland. On April 7 he even threatened to bolt the conference, letting it be known that he had ordered the waiting *George Washington* prepared for an immediate return to America. Although some sneers circulated that Wilson was behaving like a small boy who runs home to mother when thwarted, the threat had beneficial effects — Clemenceau accepted a compromise. France received the right to occupy bridgeheads along the Rhine River for fifteen years and the Rhineland was to be demilitarized to a distance of fifty kilometers east of the river. As for the Saar, France obtained use of the valuable coal mines and a customs union for fifteen years. The area would be administered by a League commission, and a plebiscite would be held after fifteen years to determine whether the Saar should return to Germany or be incorporated into France. In compensation for receiving less than France had sought, bilateral security treaties were concluded among the three powers. Clemenceau, undoubtedly aware that the American Senate might reject the security pact, protected France through a clause in the general peace treaty which permitted a prolonged occupation of the Rhenish bridgeheads beyond the specified fifteen years under certain conditions. He was thereby enabled to defend to the French parliament the acceptance of less than had been desired in regard to the Rhine frontier.

The treaties signed between Britain and France and the United States and France promised assistance if Germany should endanger French security by launching an aggressive attack on France. The two treaties would go into effect only if ratified by both Great Britain and the United States. Although the pacts were speedily approved by the British and French legislative bodies, the American Senate's failure to ratify the Franco-American treaty in effect negated British approval. Lansing, Bliss, White, and other members of the American commission were opposed to the assistance treaty because it appeared to be contrary to the collective security principles of the League Covenant. The security treaties granted France a favored status in protection against aggression and seemed to create a new triple alliance to dominate Europe and control the League. Secretary Lansing also predicted that the pact would arouse a torrent of isolationist criticism in America and would be rejected. Wilson, however, viewed the unprecedented treaty as merely a temporary expedient to reassure and protect France until the League could begin to function. The treaty with France specifically provided that it could be terminated by the League Council when that body believed that the League could assure security to France. Wilson therefore did not envision it as a permanent military alliance or as an Anglo-American-French directorate to control the postwar world.

The treaty of guarantee was a reasonable effort to assuage

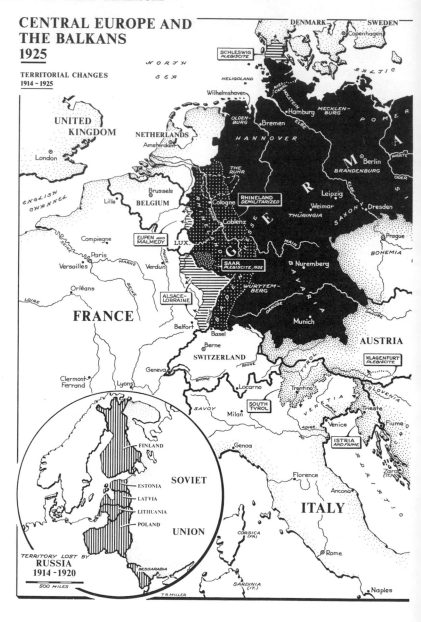

CENTRAL EUROPE AND
THE BALKANS
1925

TERRITORIAL CHANGES
1914 – 1925

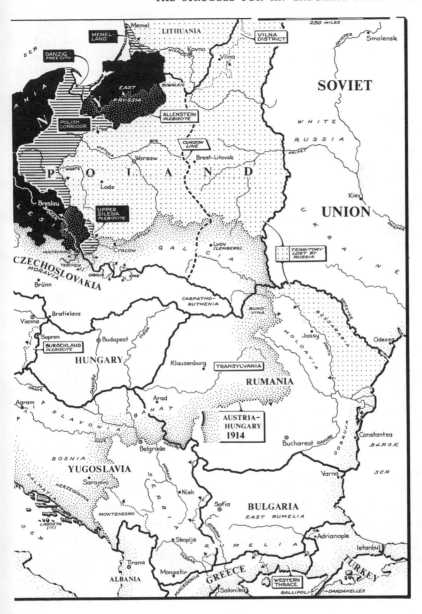

French fears and to achieve a better peace. Perhaps the president should have been more apprehensive about the reaction in the Senate, but he very reasonably assumed that if the American people accepted the League they would not balk at temporary security arrangements. In fact several important Republicans, including Senator Lodge, were favorably inclined toward such pacts and apparently would have preferred them as a substitute for the League, to preserve the new status-quo without a diminution of American sovereignty. Editorial opinion in America seemed to be evenly divided on the advisability of the assistance treaty. It never was fully debated, however, and certainly not on its merits, because of the inflamed passions characterizing the greater struggle over the Versailles Treaty. Senate rejection of the latter, consequently, doomed the security treaty as well.

II

The reparations settlement is generally conceded to have been one of Wilson's major defeats at Paris. The American delegation was committed to limiting assessments against Germany to civilian damages and to the determination of a fixed sum based on estimated capacity to pay over a limited and reasonable period of time. If payments could be restricted to a period of not more than thirty years, it was believed that reparations could be held to a feasible and fair amount. France was determined to squeeze the maximum sum from the prostrate foe, not only to secure revenge but to render Germany powerless in the future. In addition, France needed far more capital than it could raise easily for a speedy reconstruction of the areas devastated by the German invasion. Unfortunately, Anglo-American harmony broke down on this issue. The British public, as those in the other Allied countries, had visions of a rich golden harvest to be garnered from the defeated enemy. In the 1918 elections, members of Lloyd George's coalition ministry had felt it necessary to exploit the general mood of hate and greed, and had made extravagant promises of the sums to be secured. At the conference, therefore, the British and other Allied delegations were under great popular pressures to extract as much of the total costs of the war as possible from Germany.

The American delegates won the first round of the reparations battle but they lost the campaign. In the discussions in the Reparations Commission, the Allies sought to include general war costs within the civilian damages specified by the Pre-Armistice Agreement and spoke of amounts to be extracted in excess of 100 billion dollars. The Americans insisted that such astronomical figures were wholly unrealistic and ruled out general war costs as contrary to the promises made to Germany. A formula was offered and accepted whereby Article 231 of the final treaty held Germany and her allies theoretically and morally responsible for the entire costs of the war — the war guilt clause — but Article 232 limited actual reparations to civilian damages. Other provisions also authorized trial of Kaiser Wilhelm for alleged war crimes, although he was to escape prosecution.

Most of the other concessions, however, were made by the United States. Wilson was persuaded by British arguments, effectively presented by General Smuts whom he admired and trusted, to include military pensions and separation allowances as allowable civilian damages. Britain feared that otherwise it would receive little from Germany while the bulk of the indemnities would go to war-ravaged France and Belgium. When some of his experts reproached him for this departure from the logic of the Pre-Armistice Agreement, the harried president exclaimed, "I don't give a damn for logic. I am going to include pensions!" [1] Apparently he then expected the treaty to set a definite sum to be charged Germany and he did not care how it was divided among the claimants. Unfortunately, subsequent concessions, which Colonel House made during Wilson's brief illness, abandoned the effort to fix a specific amount in the treaty and to set a time limit for payments. Instead, a Reparations Commission was to be created to determine the total charges based on claims rather than on Germany's capacity to

---

[1] T. W. Lamont, "Reparations," in E. M. House and C. Seymour, eds., *What Really Happened at Paris* (New York: Scribner, 1921), 272.

pay. The addition of pensions more than doubled the indemnities assessed against Germany, which the commission in 1921 computed at thirty-three billion dollars.

Wilson's retreat probably would have been less serious if the United States had ratified the Treaty and had played its expected role on the Reparations Commission. Germans bitterly resented being saddled with sole accountability for the war under Article 231. Subsequently, many historians in England and America agreed with them that it was preposterous to attribute all responsibility to Germany and Austria for initiating the conflict. The reparations settlement was also denounced as a violation of the Pre-Armistice Agreement and as impossible to pay. Whatever the actual capacity of Germany to meet the obligations imposed by the commission, in fact it was to remit only a small part of the total.

In redrawing the map of postwar Europe, the American and British delegations were generally in agreement and worked for boundaries based primarily upon ethnic considerations. Conversely, France supported the creation of a big Poland, Czechoslovakia, and Roumania as potential allies with which to check German power in eastern and central Europe. Wilson and Lloyd George had to recognize economic and strategic factors, of course, but they did make a great effort to adhere to principles of nationality, on the grounds of justice and of a lasting settlement. The Americans were more sympathetic to Polish aspirations than were the British and supported the claims of the new state for a corridor to the Baltic Sea through German territory and the annexation of the German-inhabited port of Danzig. When Lloyd George strongly condemned the proposed line as a violation of German nationality, Wilson and the American experts defended it as economically and strategically necessary. A compromise was achieved through the designation of Danzig. When Lloyd George strongly condemned the proposed nomically with Poland. The eastern frontiers of Poland were not settled at the same time because of the absence of Russia from the conference, one more indication of the unfortunate results of the failure at Paris to achieve a solution to the Russian problem. Insofar as seemed feasible, the boundaries of Roumania and Greece were drawn along ethnic lines, whereas

Czechoslovakia was allocated the heavily German-inhabited areas on the borders of Bohemia in order to give the new state a natural defensive frontier against Germany. Fully aware that the settlement did not and could not entirely conform to the principle of self-determination, Wilson and Lloyd George cooperated in a successful effort to impose treaties for the protection of minorities upon the new states. When the minority treaties were protested as a violation of sovereignty, Wilson reasonably replied that since the primary responsibility for the preservation of peace rested upon the major powers, they must insist upon the elimination of potential dangers to that peace.

Under the terms of the secret Treaty of London Italy laid claim to the Trentino and Austrian-inhabited South Tyrol. President Wilson was persuaded that Italy needed the South Tyrol for strategic reasons and readily consented, despite the principle of self-determination. He also conceded the acquisition of Trieste and most of Istria on the Adriatic Sea. But when Italy made a determined bid for the port city of Fiume and the Dalmatian coast south of the Istrian peninsula, the American president balked. The Allies in the Treaty of London in effect had reserved Fiume for Serbia, the nucleus of the new state of Yugoslavia. Wilson's Fourteen Points had also promised the South Slavs an adequate outlet on the Adriatic Sea. With Trieste already conceded to Italy, acquisition of Fiume would have left Yugoslavia without a major port. In addition, although the core of the city was inhabited by Italians, the suburbs and surrounding areas were overwhelmingly Slavic in population. This was also true of Dalmatia. For these reasons, Wilson was determined in his rejection of the Italian claims.

The inevitable deadlock ensued. Anxious to avoid alienating Italy, Colonel House suggested a very complicated arrangement which would have given Italy eastern Istria and established a League trusteeship over Fiume and northern Dalmatia. With a few exceptions, the American commissioners and advisers were unanimous in condemnation of the proposed compromise. Lansing expressed the opinion of many when he exclaimed to House's emissary that the plan "would never work, that I was utterly sick of these impossible compromises, that there had been far too much of it, and that we were simply sowing future wars by not standing rigidly by principle." [2] Orlando rejected such plans in any case as inadequate in terms of the defense needs of Italy.

The president needed little encouragement to remain firm in his opposition. Perhaps he regretted the earlier concessions to Italy and now sought to make amends. He could not perceive any valid economic or strategic reasons why Italy should receive Fiume and Dalmatia. To force Premier Orlando and his government to retreat, Wilson resorted to a technique he had often used successfully at home. He would appeal over the heads of Orlando and his ministers to the Italian people who had recently cheered him with abandon and whose innate sense of justice he hoped to arouse. Unfortunately, he neither understood the nationalistic mood of the Italians nor could he manipulate the situation as he desired. His public statement, therefore, despite its well-reasoned arguments, was a serious blunder. Orlando did not permit its publication in Italy until his own defense was ready for release. In the interval he left the conference and returned home to appeal to the inflamed nationalism of his people. He of course received an overwhelming endorsement of his position. How Wilson could have expected a different outcome has long puzzled students of the conference. The episode revealed once again his rather inflexible attitude of moral rectitude and his messianic sense of mission.

The repercussions of the Fiume clash further weakened Wilson's position at the conference. Since Lloyd George and Clemenceau had agreed with him on this issue, the president had hoped that they would give him public support and face Italy with a united front. Those two statesmen, however, chose to remain in the background while Wilson bore the onus of refusing Italy's demands. Perhaps the way thus was eased for Italy's subsequent return to the conference, for Orlando came back after an absence of ten days; meanwhile Wilson received the anger of the Italian people. In addition, Wilson's firm stand alienated large numbers of Italian-American voters in the United States and provided additional maneuvering room for his domestic critics. Finally, it turned out to have been

---

[2] April 17, 1919, Lansing Desk Diary.

a largely futile defense of principle in any case, for Italy subsequently (1920 and 1924) imposed its own solution on the weaker Yugoslav state.

III

Japan had three major aims at the Paris conference: adoption of a racial equality clause, recognition of its legal title to the former German islands in the North Pacific, and approval of the transfer to Japan of the German holdings in Shantung Province, China. Success was achieved on all save the racial equality clause and President Wilson thereby experienced what seemed to be one of his most serious reverses in the struggle for a peace based on the Fourteen Points.

It has often been assumed that the Japanese made their request for a racial equality clause in the peace treaty primarily for bargaining purposes. It could be used to embarrass the western powers, for after the inevitable opposition was aroused Japan could accept rejection in exchange for success with its more substantial claims. Recent studies have revealed, however, that the Japanese government sincerely sought the inclusion of an article in the Covenant which would recognize the principle of racial equality. Because of its wartime understandings with the Allies and treaties with China, the Tokyo government initially expected little difficulty in obtaining the islands and Shantung. Japan had long resented immigration restrictions by the United States and the British Dominions directed at Orientals. The American delegation was not averse to the equality proposal but the British Commonwealth delegates were, especially Prime Minister Hughes of Australia. Hughes threatened, by inference, to appeal to the anti-Japanese element in the United States, particularly strong in the western states, if Wilson persisted in support of the proposed declaration. The clause was finally rejected in the Commission on the League by a vote of eleven for and six abstentions; President Wilson, who presided, abstained from the vote and ruled that the proposal had failed to secure the unanimity necessary for adoption. Racial prejudice and political fears of angry reactions

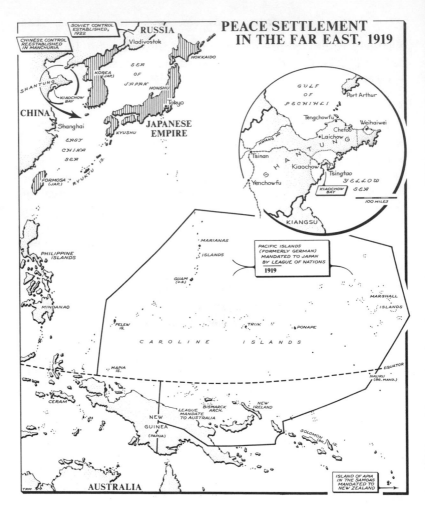

PEACE SETTLEMENT IN THE FAR EAST, 1919

at home, to which Wilson obviously was not immune, prevented a much needed affirmation of the basic equality of all men.

Rejection of the racial equality clause no doubt made it more difficult to oppose the other Japanese demands. Japan in fact experienced little trouble in securing title to the North Pacific islands, although as Class C mandates held under League supervision. Despite some concern by the War and Navy Departments about the strategic dangers of Japan controlling chains of islands lying athwart American communication lines between the Philippine Islands and Hawaii, and a desire for cable landing rights on the island of Yap, Wilson and Secretary Lansing were relatively unconcerned about the practical effects of the acquisitions. The United States settled for the mandate solution that presumably safeguarded its strategic interests by the provisions prohibiting fortification of the islands.

Shantung was a much more serious problem which threatened to disrupt the conference. An ominous clash of will ensued between the American and the Japanese delegations, resolved only by Wilson's capitulation in the closing days of the peace conference.

When the European war began, Japan exploited the altered power situation in the Far East to seize the German leasehold in the Chinese province of Shantung. Subsequently, during and after the infamous Twenty-One Demands crisis in 1915, the Japanese government compelled the weak and divided Chinese government not only to recognize the transfer but to enlarge the concessions thus obtained. By 1919 Japan had extended operations well beyond the German sphere of a fifty-mile radius around the Kiao-chow leasehold and was garrisoning troops into the interior at the termini of the Tsingtao-Tsinan Railway. President Wilson and Secretary Bryan registered formal American reservations in the *caveat* of May 1915. The United States would not recognize Sino-Japanese agreements impairing American treaty rights or the principles of the Open Door Policy in China.

When Lansing became secretary of state, he brought to the office a well-matured and practical approach to Far Eastern problems. He interpreted the traditional Open Door Policy in the narrower sense of economic equality of opportunity for all foreigners in China and, unlike Wilson, he was less interested in efforts to uphold Chinese integrity and independence. He entertained great hopes for expanded commercial and industrial opportunities for American capital in China. At the same time he understood Japan's vital economic and strategic interests in its huge neighbor and the greater military and naval power which Japan was able to exert there. He envisioned the problem, consequently, as one of avoiding acute Japanese-American rivalry through an agreement which would still protect essential American interests in China. During the Twenty-One Demands crisis, he had proposed to Bryan and Wilson a "bargain" whereby the United States government would recognize Japan's special interests in southern Manchuria, Inner Mongolia, and Shantung, in exchange for the cessation of protests over American immigration and alien land laws, and reassurances that the Open Door principles would be defined and observed within the Japanese spheres of influence. The president, apparently for moral reasons, declined to make the attempt and instead adopted the firmer line of the May *caveat.*

After the American entry into war, Lansing returned to thoughts of a special arrangement safeguarding American economic interests in China proper but conceding Japan's preeminent role in Manchuria and Mongolia. He was convinced that the moderate elements within the island empire would welcome such a solution, but he feared that an unyielding American attitude would encourage Japanese extremism and efforts to control all China. The secretary was no longer willing to concede Shantung to Japan, however, for the State Department had encouraged renewed economic activity by American firms in the area — a type of revived dollar diplomacy — and Lansing hoped that these enterprises together with projected reorganization loans to the Chinese government would destroy all spheres within China south of the Great Wall. Subsequently, Wilson approved an effort to revive the old International Bankers Consortium as a means of providing needed funds to the Chinese government and preventing an exclusive dependence upon Japanese capital. Presumably Japan would be willing to abandon political rights in Shantung, while retaining the German economic holdings, in return for recognition of its other interests.

Intimations were received in the spring of 1917 that the Japanese government would welcome an understanding with the United States. By this time Japan had secured arrangements with the principal Allied powers recognizing its gains in the Far East and understandably was anxious for a similar agreement with the American government. Lansing was eager to reach an accord, particularly since rumors were circulating of a possible Japanese-German understanding that would disturb the Far Eastern balance. Because his own relations with the president were then rather strained, the evidence indicates that the secretary tried to work indirectly through Colonel House. The colonel seems to have been readily persuaded of the necessity for such an attempt, for he replied to Lansing that "I have been very much concerned over our relations with that country. Not so much at the moment, but what the future holds. . . . [I]f care is not taken, trouble is certain." [3] Subsequently, he warned the president that "unless we make some concessions in regard to her sphere of influence in the East, trouble is sure, sooner or later[,] to come." [4]

Even House, however, could not persuade Wilson of the necessity for a compromise. The president remained determined to oppose all spheres of influence in China and to uphold Chinese integrity by vigorous diplomacy. As a consequence, when the special Japanese war mission led by Viscount Kikujiro Ishii arrived in the fall of 1917, a mutually satisfactory arrangement was impossible. In vain Japan sought recognition of its paramount interests, political and economic, in China and especially in Manchuria, while Lansing at Wilson's directions was compelled to refuse and instead to condemn all spheres in China. The result was the Lansing-Ishii Agreement of November 1917, an agreement not to agree phrased in ambiguous yet courteous diplomatic terminology. While Japan's undefined "special interests," rather than the "paramount interests" Ishii had sought, were recognized in China and particularly in areas contiguous to Japanese possessions, the territorial integrity of China and observance of the Open Door Policy were reaffirmed. A secret protocol in effect pledged both nations not to take advantage of the war to obtain special advantages in China at the expense of other interested powers.

The two governments interpreted the agreement differently. Japan construed recognition of special interests to mean paramount political and economic interests, whereas the State Department insisted that the phrase had meant no more than that Japan had a close geographical relationship with China. Probably the Japanese interpretation was sounder in terms of traditional diplomatic usage, but the important fact was that Wilson had re-

---

[3] House to Lansing, June 27, 1917, House Papers.
[4] House to Wilson, September 18, 1918, House Papers.

fused to bargain and insisted upon a Japanese retreat from China.

As Burton F. Beers has noted in a stimulating study of the period, the historian must ask if the United States had not missed a significant turning point in its relations with Japan. If an agreement could have been made along the lines contemplated by Lansing, Japanese and American interests would have been at least temporarily satisfied and yet China's national existence apparently would have been strengthened rather than weakened. China had not exercised actual control over such peripheral areas as Manchuria for years. Manchuria in a sense was an undeveloped frontier whose fate in the first half of the twentieth century apparently resided with Russia and Japan, not China. Lansing's proposed compromise would have recognized that fact in return for safeguards for China proper. Unlike President Wilson, he apparently realized that Japan had both greater interests and greater available power to exert in the Far East than had the United States. Wilson's course of moral condemnation of Japanese expansion did not alter the realities of the situation; it merely set the stage for a painful confrontation at Paris.

In the interval prior to the convening of the peace conference, Lansing agreed with Wilson that Japan should be compelled to restore Shantung to China. His reasons, however, were different. Although the president continued to feel a moral imperative to oppose Japan in China, the secretary apparently was still persuaded that an understanding with Tokyo was possible. Nevertheless, he feared that the militarists were securing a dominant position within the Japanese government, and that a firm stand on Shantung was necessary to encourage Japanese moderates to reassert control and thereby restore the basis for an agreement. The other commissioners at Paris, with the exception of House, also supported a firm policy in regard to Shantung. House, practical-minded as always, believed that there was no reasonable prospect of success in such an effort and he was apprehensive of increased Japanese-American antagonism.

Japan presented a strong legal case to the Council of Ten in Paris, claiming Shantung on the basis of conquest and treaties made with China in 1915 and 1918. Furthermore, Great Britain and France were constrained by previous agreements to support the Japanese contentions. The principle of self-determination, though invoked, did not really apply to the issue. There never was any suggestion that China did not possess theoretical sovereignty over the area. The Americans did have good reason to believe, however, that in practice Chinese control had been seriously impaired by the expanded political and military operations of Japan beyond the confines of the former German leasehold. Consequently, the Chinese delegation was given much American aid and sympathy in presenting its case that China's entry into the war had canceled the German concessions which then had reverted to the Chinese nation. The treaties with Japan, relating to the transfer of the holdings, were denounced by the Chinese delegates as the product of coercion and hence invalid.

President Wilson initially requested that Japan, in accordance with the Chinese claims, simply restore the area to China. When that failed, he proposed a face-saving solution whereby Germany would cede its former possessions to the Allied and Associated powers, who would act as trustees until final disposition. Japan rejected these proposals and insisted upon retention of its rights gained by conquest and sanctioned by treaty. Its delegation let it be known that unless the peace treaty formally transferred the German holdings to Japan, the delegation would not sign the peace nor would Japan participate in the League of Nations. President Wilson saw no way out of the dilemma except surrender. The Italian delegation had already walked out of the conference and it was feared might not return, while Russia and Germany would not be within the League. If Japan left the conference, an ominous alliance between Japan, outcast Russia, and defeated Germany seemed only too likely. Even more important to the president was the fear that the League of Nations, in his view mankind's best hope, might be moribund as the result of these defections.

The decision to capitulate was Wilson's own. He did consult his fellow commissioners and received the advice of Lansing, Bliss, and White to stand firm on the issue. Lansing used his talents in a vain effort at persuading the Japanese to accept a compromise. When that proved impossible, however, he and the other two commissioners advised resistance even if Japan did bolt the conference. In fact, Lansing believed that the Japanese were merely bluffing, that Japan's role as a great power was so new and its position sufficiently precarious that it would not dare affront world opinion by refusing to sign the Treaty and join the League. Subsequent studies have indicated that he was much too sanguine and that Wilson's apprehensions were well founded. House, on the other hand, counseled compliance with the Japanese demands. In accepting that solution, Wilson was consoled by an unsigned Japanese promise to retain only the economic holdings of Germany in Shantung while restoring political and military control to China at an unspecified future date.

The reactions at Paris and abroad were sharp and angry. The Chinese delegation was naturally disappointed and declined to sign the Versailles Treaty. Many idealistic Chinese were most disappointed with the American prophet from whom so much had been expected. Lansing privately branded the president's decision "a calamity and an abandonment of principle." [5] Bliss and White were also deeply depressed and there was talk of resigning or refusing to sign the Treaty. In America the response of many observers, including many heretofore ardent Wilsonians, was one of great disillusionment and condemnation of an apparent compromise with imperialism. Critics distorted the concession to mean an abandonment of thirty or forty million Chinese to Japanese rule and sovereignty. The Shantung settlement, together with Article X of the Covenant, was to be one of the most criticized aspects of the Versailles Treaty in the subsequent debates before the American public. Yet Wilson's retreat had been a realistic acceptance of the inevitable. He had come to realize at last that Japan could not be evicted from Shantung except by a use of force, which neither he nor the American people were willing to do. Mere moral condemnation of Japan, by refusing to accede to its demands, would have achieved nothing and perhaps would have destroyed or further weakened the League of Nations. Unfortunately, the president's decision was too late for the maximum gain. If he had permitted Lansing earlier to reach an understanding with Japan on Shantung and Manchuria, the entire controversy probably could have been avoided or reduced in intensity. As it was, Japan appeared to have won a great victory at Wilson's expense. Ironically, in

---

[5] April 30, 1919, Lansing Desk Diary.

view of the criticism aimed at Wilson, Japan kept its promise and in 1922 restored the Shantung leasehold to Chinese control.

IV

On May 7, the fourth anniversary of the sinking of the *Lusitania,* the formal peace conference began when the bulky Treaty was handed to the representatives of vanquished Germany. At the Trianon Palace at Versailles, before the assembled delegates, Clemenceau curtly informed the German chief delegate, Count Brockdorff-Rantzau, that Germany had asked for peace and the Allies were now ready to give it; fifteen days would be allowed for study of the document, then the German delegates might submit in writing whatever observations they deemed appropriate. The subsequent Germany reply raised numerous objections to the proposed terms and charged violation of the Pre-Armistice Agreement in regard to territorial losses, reparations, and unilateral disarmament. Although a few relatively minor changes were made, the victorious powers insisted that the Treaty be accepted without further delay or the war would be resumed and Allied armies would march into the heart of Germany. With all avenues of escape closed, the new German republic reluctantly ordered its delegates to sign the dictated peace.

On the appointed day, June 28, an impressive tableau was staged in the Hall of Mirrors at Versailles. Throngs of delegates, visitors, and newsmen overflowed the room and the surrounding gardens. When Lansing arrived for the ceremony, a smiling Clemenceau greeted him with the remark, "This is a great day for France"; the premier then insisted on grasping both of the secretary's hands, for "that is the way France and America should greet each other today." [6] Upon the arrival of Wilson and Lloyd George, and after the autograph seekers had been satisfied, the two obscure German representatives entered the hall and affixed their signatures to the Treaty. The American and Allied

---

[6] Lansing Memorandum, June 28, 1919, U. S. State Department, *Papers Relating to the Foreign Relations of the United States, 1919: the Paris Peace Conference,* XI, 599.

delegations then followed in the signing. President Wilson sub-sequently admitted to Lansing that he had been so excited by the high drama of the moment that his hand had trembled when attaching his signature. Within an hour the signing was completed and to the thunderous cheers of the waiting multitude the greatest peace conference since the Congress of Vienna had reached its climax. Treaties still remained to be concluded with the other Central powers, but as far as the United States was concerned those were less dramatic and absorbing tasks. That evening, President Wilson bade Paris farewell and departed for America bearing the Treaty with its Covenant of the League of Nations.

Debate about the nature of the Versailles Treaty began even before it had been completed. Many disillusioned idealists branded it a Carthaginian peace, dictated to the beaten foe and designed to keep Germany prostrate indefinitely. Germany was stripped of its colonies, navy, and merchant marine; deprived of extensive territories inhabited by Germans, in violation of the principle of self-determination; and forced to acknowledge its war guilt while assuming the burden of large but as yet un-fixed reparations. Moreover, Germany alone was to be disarmed and left to the mercy of a vengeful France. Why, many asked, had the Fourteen Points been so flagrantly violated? The answer of some critics was expressed by John Maynard Keynes, a British economist at the peace conference and a former admirer of Wilson. In *The Economic Consequences of the Peace*, published in 1920, Keynes attributed the failure to Wilson's moral collapse at Paris. The philosopher-king from the West, he wrote, had turned out to be merely a stubborn Presbyterian theologian in politics, whose very rigidity of mind and lack of detailed preparation had rendered him vulnerable to the agilities of Lloyd George and the cynical determination of Clemenceau. The president had been confused and deceived by these adept Old World leaders and, obsessed with his dream of a league of nations, had sacrificed most of his own Fourteen Points. After the outbreak of World War II, scholars became less concerned with whether Wilson had achieved all that was possible in behalf of a liberal peace and instead began to criticize the Wilsonian peace program as too idealistic for the painful realities of the modern world. George F. Kennan, in a series of stimulating lectures on American diplomacy since 1900, summed up the view of the realists who deplored the marriage of war hysteria and utopian idealism with which Wilson and his fellow Americans had turned World War I into a holy crusade for a world without conflict and injustice.

The judgment of most students of the period, however, is that neither the disillusioned liberals nor the realistic critics have presented a balanced and fair appraisal of Wilson's efforts at Paris. It was true that the Wilsonian peace program was highly idealistic and was only sketchily outlined in his wartime addresses. Yet that which in the abstract appears visionary sometimes can be eminently practical in application. Thus the principle of self-determination, regardless of the many difficulties in applying it to concrete cases, expressed the realization that any peace treaty which did not accord a very large measure of satisfaction to nationalistic aspirations was doomed to an early demise. Wilson realized, perhaps not as much as he should have, that he would experience great difficulty in implementing his goals against the more narrowly conceived national interests of the Allies at the peace conference. Far from being unprepared, he had created a body of scholars, the Inquiry, to gather information and suggest solutions for the problems likely to arise at the peacemaking.

At Paris, Wilson drove himself almost to the point of exhaustion in conscientious application to the tasks of the conference. He consistently revealed a depth of knowledge and understanding beyond that of his counterparts, Lloyd George, Orlando, and Clemenceau. In retrospect, he appears to have been far more realistic than Clemenceau in his opposition to excessive reparations and efforts to dismember Germany, and the same was true of his objections to many of the boundary changes proposed by the various powers at the conference. Wilson undoubtedly was an idealist at Paris, but he combined with idealism a high degree of practicality and stood firmly for a reasonable and workable peace.

The Versailles Treaty was harsh in many of its provisions and it definitely fell short of a complete realization of the liberal peace goals. Wilson had experienced a defeat in the reparations settlement, though he hoped that American participation in the commission which would determine the actual amount Germany would pay could keep the total bill to a reasonable level. Only Germany was disarmed, but the Covenant of the League did pledge future efforts at significant general reductions. The demilitarization and occupation of the Rhineland and French exploitation of the Saar Valley seemed draconian in German eyes, yet France in view of the past was entitled to reasonable safeguards against a renewed invasion. Moreover, Wilson had successfully defended his principles when he and Lloyd George dissuaded France from insisting on the dismemberment of Germany. The peace undoubtedly would have had an even poorer prospect of permanence if German nationalism had been affronted by partition.

Self-determination, although necessarily transgressed in certain areas because of the intermixtures of population and considerations of economic and strategic factors, was generally honored in the drawing of the boundaries of the new states. Italy had been conceded some areas not inhabited by a majority of Italians, but Wilson had resisted the claim to Fiume, vital to the new state of Yugoslavia, even to the point of an open rupture with the Italian delegation. As for Shantung, it was more an apparent than a real defeat, whatever the political repercussions in America. The mandate solution for Germany's colonies in one sense only put a respectable facade over their acquisition by the victors; yet the new system subjected the mandatory powers to legal and moral restrictions and it symbolized the end of the era of nineteenth-century imperialism. Finally, Wilson undoubtedly regarded the creation of the League of Nations as more than justifying all the defeats and compromises at Paris. Whatever the defects of that global collective security organization which time was to reveal — it broke down in the 1930's primarily because it was not supported — it did offer man's best hope for a more secure and progressive world and it would probably not have been achieved, or at least not then, without the American president's determined efforts. A peace admittedly less than perfect would be preserved and improved, Wilson hoped, through the operations of the League.

CHAPTER X

The Defeat of the Treaty

THE *George Washington* arrived off the American coast on July 8. Upon debarking, President Wilson spoke briefly at Carnegie Hall in New York City about his work at Paris. On July 10 he personally delivered the 264-page Treaty of Peace with Germany to the Senate. His reception was in sharp contrast to the scene a little over two years before when he had presented his war message. Then he had been cheered enthusiastically and after his speech, spoken to an audience intent on his every word, Senator Henry Cabot Lodge had shaken his hand and warmly congratulated him: "Mr. President, you have expressed in the loftiest manner possible the sentiments of the American people."[1] Now, although the Democratic members gave him a ringing ovation, the Republican senators with few exceptions received the address in grim silence. Apparently reacting to the undertone of hostility in the chamber, the president was not at his best. He dropped several words from his typed manuscript and spoke of the Treaty merely in generalized terms. Only when he referred to the League of Nations did a note of eloquence and feeling suffuse his remarks. He seemed to be speaking to an audience beyond the Senate when he described the League as "the practical statesman's hope of success." As he concluded, he ignored the manuscript before him for a dramatic appeal to the nation:

The stage is set, the destiny disclosed. It has come about by no plan of our conceiving, but by the hand of God, who led us into this way. We cannot turn back. We can only go forward, with lifted eyes and fresh-

---

[1] April 3, 1917, *New York Times*.

ened spirit, to follow the vision. It was of this that we dreamed at our birth. America shall in truth show the way. . . .[2]

I

As Selig Adler has pointed out in his able study of isolationism, if Wilson's goals had been restricted to specific national interests he could have compromised at Paris without serious diminution of prestige, but as the advocate of a more idealistic program for peace even minor concessions damaged his reputation as moral spokesman for the world. It did little good to point out to critics that Wilson at Paris had to negotiate with able and determined leaders of other great powers whose desires could not always be denied. The ideal rarely can be entirely achieved; at Paris it had been a question of an imperfect treaty based on compromise or none at all. Probably Wilson should have done more during the war to persuade the American people that in addition to idealistic purposes they did have important national self-interests involved in the struggle, though admittedly not of a territorial or economic nature. It perhaps also would have been wise to have made the people aware that the Allied powers had definite territorial and financial goals of their own which were not necessarily evil or to be entirely frustrated at the peace table. Even more necessary, it would appear, would have been a concerted campaign by Wilson and his administration to discuss the finished Treaty before the public in terms of enlightened self-interest: the utility of the League of Nations in promoting an end to costly land and naval armaments; the protection offered by collective security against revival of German and Russian imperialism, with perhaps some intimations in regard to Japan; the justice and convenience to be provided by a world court and international law codified under League encouragement; and the variety of useful and practical nonpolitical functions to be sponsored by the League. The League of Nations could have been defended as the best prescription for an orderly and prosperous world in which the United States could flourish

---

[2] *Congressional Record*, 66th Congress, 2d Session, Vol. 58, 2336–2339.

in peace and security. Although Wilson did refer to these more practical benefits, he continued to place too great an emphasis on moral and idealistic exhortations which were losing their appeal to a jaded and increasingly disillusioned people.

There was a growing mood of apathy or hostility on the part of many citizens to membership in the League of Nations. As a people, Americans traditionally have taken little interest in foreign affairs except during times of acute crises. After the Armistice, there was a tendency for private affairs once more to take precedence. People were tiring of crusades, idealism, and European distresses. This mood was deepened by the problems of the postwar reconversion of industry and agriculture and the demobilization of the armed services. The war also had engendered intense nationalism, as the wartime anti-German hysteria in America had attested: censorship, local committees of public safety, spy scares, and efforts to suppress German music, literature, and even the teaching of the language. It was only to be expected that this war-stimulated chauvinism should continue into the postwar era in the form of an aroused or superpatriotism. Nationalists urged their fellow citizens to remember Washington's farewell address: American sovereignty must not be diminished by membership in the League superstate; the sacred Monroe Doctrine should not be weakened; and the United States should preserve full freedom to pursue its own interests and regulate its own affairs. Fear also was expressed that the League might nullify the American tariff and prevent restriction of immigration, thereby opening the country to ruinous intrusions of foreign goods and people. Many Americans evidently had never really become convinced internationalists in more than a superficial sense. The isolationist tradition remained strong, particularly where reenforced by ethnic and political factors as in the middle western states. There large numbers of German and Scandinavian-Americans sympathized with Germany and denounced the Versailles Treaty as unjust. Midwestern agrarian opinion, already inclined to distrust British bankers and eastern industrialists as the source of agriculture's woes, tended to attribute the war to the profit-mad desires of the bankers and munitions makers.

The impact of isolationist sentiment, popular disillusionment, and heightened nationalism was increased by the alienation of the hyphenates. The United States contained millions of people either born in Europe or with one or both parents as immigrants. Many of these retained a degree of loyalty or emotional commitment to the mother country and reacted angrily to various provisions of the Versailles Treaty. Numerous Irish-Americans, traditionally adherents of the Democratic Party, were estranged by the failure of the Paris conference to force Great Britain to grant Ireland its freedom, and by the six votes which the British Empire and Commonwealth secured in the League Assembly. Italian-Americans were strongly inclined to support Italy in the controversy over Fiume and to feel that the mother country had fared ill in the division of booty at Paris, while German-Americans were embittered at the punitive features of the peace treaty. These discontented groups provided attractive opportunities for political angling by the Republican leadership in the struggle over approval of the peace treaty.

The desertion of many "liberals" was a very serious loss to Wilson and the Democratic Party in the fight over the Treaty. Many advocates of progressive reform and political independents had moved into Wilson's camp and had helped provide the margin of victory for his reelection in 1916. Most had supported the entry into war only with great reluctance and in the belief that it was a crusade for justice and a lasting peace. Their hopes exalted by Wilsonian oratory, liberals expected that the achievement of victory would signal the abolition of balances of power and alliances, the supplanting of secret diplomacy with democratic methods of conducting foreign relations, and the relegation of imperialism to past history. Unprepared for the clash of self-interest and ideals which occurred at Paris and the inevitable compromises that had to be made, many of these supporters were speedily alienated from Wilson's camp. The Versailles Treaty was denounced by such previously pro-Wilson journals as the *New Republic* and *The Nation* as not a peace but a blueprint for future wars and a betrayal of expectations for a just settlement. The financial exactions imposed on Germany were condemned by disillusioned critics as vindictive and as a violation of the spirit of the Fourteen Points and the provisions of the Pre-Armistice Agreement; while the territorial clauses involving the South Tyrol, the Saar Basin, occupation of the Rhineland, Shantung, and the disposition of the German colonies were censured as old-fashioned imperialism violating the principle of the self-determination of peoples. The League of Nations, desirable though it might be under other circumstances, was also opposed because it sanctioned imperialism and was committed to the preservation of an unjust world order. It could only lead to war. The disenchanted but highly vocal liberals thus supplied valuable arguments and support to Wilson's opponents in the Senate.

Despite the growing opposition to the Treaty and the League of Nations, the evidence indicates that the majority of Americans in the summer of 1919 still supported membership in some kind of a league. Newspaper editorials and polls, speeches and popular meetings, all revealed continued approval of participation in an international organization to promote peace. The sentiment apparently was not very intense, however, as the deadlock which soon occurred in the Senate amply attested. If opinion had strongly favored membership in the League, the politicians would hardly have dared to frustrate the popular will. Opportunity was thus provided for League opponents to delay action on the Treaty while exploiting mass fears and misconceptions.

II

With public opinion in a malleable state, either unformed or lacking in intensity of conviction, the decision in the Senate apparently could have favored approval of the Treaty as easily as its rejection. That it was to be the latter can be attributed in part to a genuine disagreement over the nature of America's commitment in world affairs, and in part to an excess of political and personal partisanship. In the light of its record since 1898, Republican opposition to the Treaty and the League was not inevitable. Wilson's failures at conciliation and cooperation in foreign policy and the desires of Republican leaders for political gain were, in addition to serious doubts about the League, to contribute to leading the party into opposition and toward the isolationism of the 1920's.

The Senate which received the Treaty from President Wilson had a narrow Republican majority — the forty-nine Republicans had only a two-vote margin over the forty-seven Democrats, but that permitted them to organize the Foreign Relations Committee and to control the machinery of the Senate. The Republicans were naturally anxious to manage affairs so that victory would be assured in the 1920 presidential campaign. They were the traditional majority party and, although Wilson had won narrow victories in 1912 and 1916, the 1918 results indicated that the country was returning to its Republican allegiance. A large number of the Republican senators, and some of the Democrats as well, disliked Wilson intensely because of his alleged dictatorial manner. Wilson had greatly expanded presidential powers during the war and there was a widespread feeling in Congress that the time had come to reassert legislative prerogatives. In a very real sense the struggle over the Treaty was to be an executive-legislative conflict for control of foreign policy.

Many conservative Republicans had also been greatly disturbed by the progressive reforms enacted since 1913 and feared that the country was on the road to socialism. If the Treaty were approved without change, Wilson and the Democrats would receive the credit and could present themselves to the electorate as the party which had enacted important domestic reforms, fought the war through to victory, and then had made a peace to end wars and ensure the reign of international justice. It was feared that Wilson would even seek a third term, or at least try to establish his own political dynasty. If these unpalatable events were to be avoided, political considerations demanded that the treaty issue be handled in a way calculated to damage Wilson and strengthen the Republican Party.

The Republican majority contained three clearly discernible groups in regard to the issue of membership in the League. At one end of the spectrum were the "Irreconcilables." Numbering about fourteen members, the group comprised die-hard opponents to American membership in any kind of league. Their motives were mixed. A study of the two Irreconcilable senators from Illinois, Medill McCormick and L. Y. Sherman, has revealed that McCormick's opposition was largely based on his

pro-Irish sympathies and anglophobia, together with a nationalistic aversion to membership in a superstate league and a consequent diminution of American sovereignty. Sherman on an
earlier occasion had indicated some sympathy for the league
concept, but he subsequently moved into the opposition, partly
because of personal and political enmity for Wilson and partly
for nationalistic reasons. He too feared the League as a superstate and he discerned dangers of alleged Vatican influence and
the votes of Roman Catholic nations which might control the
new structure and use it to breach the wall of separation between church and state. William E. Borah of Idaho naively
viewed the League as a kind of international bankers' conspiracy
to dominate and plunder the world. He objected also to the
loss of diplomatic freedom which membership would entail
and insisted that America's true function was to avoid political
entanglements while setting a moral example of decency and
self-government to the world. Although only a small bloc, the
Irreconcilables had intelligent leadership and were in a key
position to delay consideration of the Treaty while public opinion was alerted to its disadvantages.

Republican "Mild Reservationists" stood at the opposite end
from the Irreconcilables. This group included a number of the
ablest and most liberal-minded Republicans in the Senate, such
as Frank B. Kellogg of Minnesota. In general they sought the
addition of a few reservations to the Treaty, to clarify certain
points, which would not seriously affect it and would not require foreign assent. The "Strong Reservationists," a larger
group, included the Republican leader Henry Cabot Lodge.
These senators wanted to append numerous amendments or
reservations to the Treaty and especially to the League Covenant. In addition, the principal Allied powers should signify
acceptance of the alterations before the United States could
participate in the League. Probably most were sincere in their
assertions that the Covenant was poorly drafted and failed to
safeguard vital American interests. The Monroe Doctrine required specific protection from League jurisdiction, it was contended, and there must be no interference with American control of tariff and immigration questions. Above all the obligation of members under Article X to uphold the integrity and

independence of other states was regarded as too sharp a departure from America's past practice of noninvolvement and as an infringement upon the constitutional powers of Congress to declare war and regulate the military establishment. The Covenant, it was claimed, would transfer a large degree of control over America's right to declare war, make peace, and maintain such armies as it chose to the new international organization. A number of Strong Reservationists believed that the positive guarantee should be scrapped and reliance instead placed upon a world court and arbitration procedures to maintain international peace.

The majority of these critics of the Covenant were not isolationists. Most were internationally minded but they were not willing to abandon American diplomatic freedom and traditions and to entrust the nation's security to the League of Nations. Arthur Link has pointed out that much of the debate over the Treaty was not between internationalists and isolationists, but between "mild internationalists" and "strong internationalists." The mild internationalists wanted to limit the degree of American involvement in the League and to avoid binding obligations under the collective security clause to defend all threatened nations. Strong internationalists or Wilsonians, which included most of the Democrats in the Senate, sought nothing less than wholehearted commitment to collective security and the assumption of the full responsibilities devolving on a great power under the Covenant. Since the Democrats could not muster even a bare majority, much less the two-thirds majority required for approval of the Treaty, political strategy seemed to require an effort to win the support of enough Republican Mild and Strong Reservationists to achieve victory.

As chairman of the Senate Foreign Relations Committee, Senator Lodge was responsible for Republican strategy on the treaty issue. He was a nationalist of the A. T. Mahan-Theodore Roosevelt type who throughout his long public career had advocated a more vigorous and responsible international role for the United States. He put his reliance, however, in a strong foreign policy supported by an adequate military posture rather than in the collective security schemes of the peace advocates. Lodge had spoken in favor of some kind of league during the war, moved by the spirit of the hour and possibly by political considerations as well. He claimed that his subsequent opposition to Wilson's League was based on the highest grounds: the Covenant was hastily and poorly drafted, and amendments or reservations were necessary to protect the Monroe Doctrine and to preclude League interference in domestic affairs. Above all, the scope and obligations of Article X had to be reduced to make it safe for America to participate. In a major speech to the Senate on August 12, 1919, Lodge forcefully stated his objections:

. . . I object in the strongest possible way to having the United States agree, directly or indirectly, to be controlled by a league which may at any time . . . be drawn in to deal with internal conflicts in other countries, no matter what those conflicts may be. . . . It must be made perfectly clear that no American soldiers . . . can ever be engaged in war or ordered anywhere except by the constitutional authorities of the United States.[3]

Whatever his doubts about the actual merits of the League, Lodge's role probably can be better understood in terms of political factors and his personal hatred for President Wilson. As the Republican leader in the Senate, it was his duty to devise a strategy which would bar Democratic gains and enhance the popular appeal of his party. He faced a difficult situation in which the Republicans in the Senate were rather sharply divided on the question of the League. The solution was to delay action while alleged defects and dangerous provisions in the Covenant were pointed out to the public, and then to present amendments or reservations designed to Republicanize the Treaty. The reservations would be framed to satisfy both Mild and Strong Reservationists, and the Irreconcilables would prefer the Treaty with these changes if it could not be defeated outright. If the president accepted the modifications, which would be the only way in which the Treaty could pass, Republicans could claim credit with the electorate for having made the Covenant safe for American membership; if Wilson refused, the onus for its rejection could be attributed to him alone.

---

[3] *Congressional Record*, 66th Congress, 2d Session, Vol. 58, 3778–3784.

On the personal level, Lodge's relationship with Wilson was marked by an obvious and well-known animosity. Each man disliked and intensely distrusted the other. The aloof and arrogant Lodge, a Ph. D. from Harvard and the author of many books, had been known as the "Scholar in Politics" until Wilson appeared on the national scene and, as a former university president and a prolific author, usurped the title. Lodge apparently viewed himself as intellectually and culturally superior to Wilson, whom he thought vastly overrated as a scholar and as a political leader. He attributed his dislike, of course, not to personal rivalry but to indications that Wilson was evasive, egotistical, and unreliable: "Mr. Wilson was devoured by the desire for power." [4] Lodge was well acquainted with the Wilson psychology and knew that the very mention of his name was enough to enrage the president. As he admitted to a colleague, he was reasonably certain that Wilson would never accept amendments or reservations to the Treaty which were popularly associated with Lodge's name. From both the political and personal points of view, the reservation strategy was a clever device well calculated for success.

III

Senator Lodge placed so many known enemies of the League of Nations on the Foreign Relations Committee that ex-President Taft accused him of deliberately "packing" it. Of the ten Republicans on the committee (to seven Democrats), six were Irreconcilables and three were Strong Reservationists. In his posthumously published account of the treaty fight, Lodge complacently described the group as "a strong committee and such as the existing conditions demanded." [5] If the Treaty had been quickly submitted to the Senate for a vote, it probably would have been approved with only minor alterations. Fully aware of that fact — some of the opponents of the League expressed

---

[4] Henry Cabot Lodge, *The Senate and the League of Nations* (New York: Scribner, 1925), 212–213.

[5] Lodge, *The Senate and the League,* 152.

to Lodge their despair at blocking eventual approval — the chairman used two weeks to read aloud the entire 264 printed pages of the text of the Treaty before a nearly empty committee room. The object clearly was to gain time for popular opposition or doubts to develop, for the document had been printed and each senator had a copy. Six weeks of public hearings followed the reading, from July 31 to September 6. Sixty witnesses took advantage of the occasion to present testimony, some of it completely irrelevant and filled with special pleading by Irish-Americans or other ethnic groups holding grievances against the Versailles Treaty. During this interval, the Irreconcilables and other critics of the League launched an intensive campaign to alert the people to the dangers of membership in the organization. Funds were contributed to the cause by a number of wealthy people, including millionaires Henry Clay Frick and Andrew Mellon. Proponents of the League were also active.

It has generally been assumed that President Wilson made only a half-hearted attempt to conciliate the Senate and that a greater effort on his part could have won sufficient support from the more moderate Republicans to secure approval of the Treaty with only mild reservations or interpretations. A study by Kurt Wimer, however, reveals that Wilson did make a serious effort to conciliate the opposition and that he indicated a readiness to accept explanatory reservations if they were not made a part of the formal act of ratification. It was true that he never had a high regard for the senatorial mentality and that he had returned from Paris weary of the compromises he had been forced to accept. He was confident that the Covenant was as nearly perfect as possible and that the American people were, or would be when fully informed, solidly in his support in the struggle with the Senate. In addition, Wilson conceived of foreign affairs as almost exclusively the responsibilty of the president, and he was inclined to view congressional efforts to alter the Treaty as invasions of presidential prerogatives which, if successful, would disturb the constitutional division of powers and responsibilities. His attitude upon his return to America, therefore, was rather unbending. He revealed this only too well when, on the day the

Treaty was presented to the Senate, he brushed aside a reporter's query about possible reservations with the curt remark that he was not going to discuss theoretical questions for the Senate was going to approve the Treaty.

Further reflection on the situation, however, soon persuaded Wilson that it would be necessary to try to win over some of his senatorial critics. Upon the urgent recommendations of his advisers, the president invited a number of Republican senators to confer with him individually at the White House. Although he tried to explain controversial features of the Treaty in a mild and reasonable manner, and indicated a receptivity to separate interpretative reservations, Wilson failed to win sufficient additional support for his cause. Several of the senators told Wilson frankly that it would be impossible to secure Senate approval without very strong reservations attached directly to the Treaty. Secretary Lansing appeared before the Senate Committee in early August and his testimony, revealing very clearly that he had been ignored at Paris, did little to strengthen the president's case. Lansing admitted the opposition he and others of the peace commission had felt in regard to the settlement of the Shantung dispute. On August 19 the Foreign Relations Committee accepted Wilson's invitation and, breaking precedent, questioned him closely for over three hours. The president patiently answered his interlocutors but again without winning any new adherents to the support of the League. He explained the Covenant clause by clause. Article X, the heart of the League, was a moral rather than a legal obligation; Congress would retain its power under the Constitution to decide questions of war and peace, and the United States was additionally protected by its veto power in the League Council. Wilson declared that he was not opposed to the attachment of interpretations by the Senate if they were not formally a part of the Treaty and did not compel its renegotiation. His critics were not satisfied and remained determined to reduce American obligations under the Covenant.

By the end of August, Wilson despaired of prompt action by the Senate and concluded that further efforts at acceptable compromise with the Republicans were futile. He decided to appeal his case to the people. He did give the Democratic minority leader, Senator Gilbert M. Hitchcock of Nebraska, four interpretative reservations relating to Article X, the exclusion of domestic questions from League jurisdiction, the Monroe Doctrine, and withdrawal from the League. These he would accept if they were not made a formal part of the Treaty. He kept his authorship a secret, however, and directed Hitchcock not to use the reservations unless necessary, for fear that any sign of compromise would only encourage his opponents to request more. The president evidently believed that none would be necessary after he had rallied the people behind his leadership. As he remarked to Lansing, who viewed the western speaking tour as a mistake, "if they [the Senate opposition] wanted war he'd 'give them a belly full.' " [6]

Although warned that the trip might do more harm than good and cautioned by his physician that his health was too frail to undertake an arduous campaign in the heat of summer, the embattled president placed his concept of duty above life itself. On September 3, his train left Washington for forty major speeches and many minor ones which would take him through the heart of the middle western states to the Pacific Coast. In one sense, the trip was a foreordained failure for even if the Democratic Party should win all the Senate seats involved in the 1920 election as the result of Wilson's campaign, it still would not command the necessary two-thirds majority to approve the Treaty unencumbered by reservations. The president could hope, however, to arouse the public so that even Republican senators not seeking reelection would bow to the popular will.

Wilson delivered over thirty major addresses prior to the forced cancellation of the remainder of his tour. His audiences were friendly and apparently receptive. Although he normally did not excel at this type of speaking and he found it an enormous drain on his energies, Wilson gave some extremely fervent and moving speeches in behalf of unqualified participation in the League of Nations. He continued to emphasize the moral obligations to promote world peace and progress, but he did make some effort to remind his audiences of the practical American stake in the success of the League. At Des Moines, for example,

---

[6] August 25, 1919, Lansing Desk Diary.

he reminded business and labor of the advantages to be gained in the more prosperous world which would result from the stabilizing influence of the League.

He also referred to the deadly disease of Communism, feeding upon disorder and theatening to spread everywhere unless checked by the creation of an orderly world society. In South Dakota he warned his audience that if the League were not successful, and he believed its success to a considerable degree depended on America willingly assuming the burdens of membership, the old balance of power system with its attendant wars would return. The United States would then have to pay a high price for security in the form of a larger military establishment, heavy taxes, and an increasing centralization of government. He repeated these warnings in subsequent speeches, but he was apparently psychologically unable to center the defense of the League on the grounds of enlightened self-interest. Instead, he repeatedly emphasized the noble task America had launched and its duty to mankind to see it through to success. The Treaty of Peace was an American-inspired settlement and the League of Nations essentialy an American type of organization. He reminded his audiences that the Covenant had already been amended to safeguard American control of domestic affairs and to protect the Monroe Doctrine; Congress alone still possessed the power over war and peace, and the Constitution was unimpaired. Finally, he defended Article X as imposing moral, rather than legal, obligations; the nation would not be automatically committed to protect the integrity of all others but would be free to act as its conscience required. To attach reservations to Article X, therefore, was unnecessary and could only weaken the mainspring of the Covenant.

After a moving address at Pueblo, Colorado, on September 25, Wilson suffered a physical breakdown. Never robust, the hardships and tensions of the tour had rapidly depleted his energies. Sleepless and wracked with severe headaches, his facial muscles twitched and it was obvious to his wife and physician that the remainder of the tour would have to be canceled. Convinced that he was beginning to arouse popular support, the exhausted president agreed only with great reluctance.

Despite rest and medication the headaches persisted after his return to Washington and, on October 2, Wilson suffered a cerebral thrombosis which paralyzed the left side of his face and body. For two weeks he was near death and for several months was almost helpless. Whether his western tour would have turned the tide in the Senate had he been able to complete it can never be known. Despite the group of Republican Irreconcilables and Strong Reservationists which followed him and attempted to counter the effect of his speeches, he had made a sufficiently favorable impression to cause his opponents considerable uneasiness. If he had retained his health, he conceivably could have returned to Washington greatly strengthened with an apparent popular mandate, to exert more effective pressure on the Senate for approval of the Treaty with few if any changes. On the other hand, the president might well have been encouraged by the results of the tour to reject all proposals for compromise, even mild reservations, and thus to have ensured a painful deadlock and defeat. In view of his physical collapse, Wilson undoubtedly would have served his cause better by remaining in the White House to maintain a close watch on the Senate and maneuver for a favorable compromise.

IV

On the tenth of September the Republican majority in the Foreign Relations Committee reported the Treaty to the Senate floor with the recommendation that forty-five amendments and four reservations should be attached to the instrument of ratification. The majority report denied charges of deliberate delay in the committee and pointed out that the other major powers had not yet ratified. The Democratic minority report reflected the president's views and requested that the Treaty be approved without change. Senator Porter J. McCumber of North Dakota, a Mild Reservationist, made a separate minority report which criticized both Republicans and Democrats for playing politics with so serious an issue. He urged prompt approval with six moderately phrased interpretive reservations. Public opinion appeared to be shifting toward approval with reservations and probably Wilson would have been well advised to have offered the Hitchcock reservations. He failed to do so, as he was then engaged in the western speaking tour which he hoped would arouse enough popular support to avoid any kind of reservations. Subsequently, his illness left the Senate Democrats virtually leaderless. When Senator Hitchcock finally offered his own version of reservations, it proved to be too late. Most moderate Republicans by then were committed to the Lodge approach and room for maneuver had been sharply restricted.

The Senate departed from tradition and debated the Treaty in public sessions. The proposed amendments were voted down as they obviously would compel renegotiation of the Treaty. On November 6 Senator Lodge abandoned them and instead introduced fourteen reservations which contained the essence of the amendments. The preamble to the Lodge Reservations required that they would have to be accepted by three of the four principal Allied signatories before Senate approval of the Treaty would go into effect. The first reservation provided that in case of withdrawal from the League of Nations the United States would be the sole judge of whether it had fulfilled the obligations required under the Covenant, and notice of withdrawal would be given by a concurrent resolution of Congress. Number two related to Article X, the mutual guarantee clause, and specified that the United States would assume no obligation to preserve the integrity of other states or to use its armed forces under the collective security provisions of the Covenant without the approval of Congress in each particular case. Number three specified that no mandate should be accepted by the United States without congressional sanction, and the fourth reserved to the nation the exclusive right to determine what were domestic questions to be excluded from League jurisdiction. The fifth refused to submit to arbitration or League action any question pertaining to the Monroe Doctrine and declared that sacred national dogma to be entirely beyond League jurisdiction and capable of interpretation only by the United States. Number six withheld approval of the treaty clauses relating to the Shantung settlement. Seven and nine prohibited financial contributions or participation in the League agencies without the approval of Congress, and number eight related to Germany and the reparations commission. The tenth reservation referred to the possible adoption of a League plan for disarmament and formally reserved the right to increase armaments if the nation were threatened by invasion. Number eleven safeguarded the right of citizens under certain conditions to continue to trade with a nation under League commercial sanctions; twelve covered claims against Germany and thirteen dealt with the power of Congress to control American participation in the International Labor Organization. The last reservation, a monument to the prevalent anglophobia, proclaimed that the American government would not be bound by any League decision or other action in which any one member had cast more than one vote.

In the interval President Wilson slowly began to regain a measure of strength. For a period he undoubtedly had been disabled within the meaning of the constitutional provisions and was completely secluded in his sickroom. Even cabinet members had been denied access to him. Secretary Lansing was convinced that it was a case of inability and that crucial domestic and foreign problems required that the vice-president should temporarily assume the duties of the chief executive. He was effectively prevented from acting by Mrs. Wilson and the White House staff, who evidently put personal loyalty to the president above the needs of the country. By November Wilson had recovered sufficiently to again supervise some of the more important functions of government. He seemed more irritable and suspicious than before and was prone to sudden weeping, but his mind was apparently as clear as ever. On the better days he could spend several hours at official business but the former energy and powers of concentration were gone. Wilson was physically impaired throughout the remainder of his term in office.

Senator Hitchcock conferred twice in November with the feeble president and gently tried to persuade him of the need for compromise with Lodge. Wilson refused; he found the Lodge Reservations completely unacceptable and wanted the responsibility for suggesting compromise left to his opponents. If the Treaty could not win approval with the Hitchcock Reservations, the president obviously preferred a deadlock in the belief that a shocked public would compel his enemies to retreat. Hitchcock concurred in this strategy and therefore must share the responsibility with the president for what ensued. According to Lansing's secondhand account, "the President said [to Hitchcock] that if the resolution of ratification was passed with the present reservations, he would withdraw the treaty." [7] Even Mrs. Wilson pleaded with Wilson to accept the Treaty with the Lodge Reservations. A number of high administration officials and Democratic members of the Senate were convinced that it could be approved in only that way and that it would be better to enter the League with the reservations than to stay out entirely. If the reservations proved crippling or objectionable to other powers, the responsibility would clearly devolve on Lodge and the Republican majority in the Senate. Wilson refused to retreat and on November 18 informed loyal Democratic senators that true friends of the Treaty would vote against the Republican-sponsored reservations. Thus on November 19 the Treaty failed to secure a two-thirds majority in any form. The vote with the Lodge Reservations was thirty-nine for and fifty-five against, with loyal Democrats following the presidential directive and joining the Irreconcilables in opposition. Without reservations, the vote was thirty-eight for and fifty-three against, and an earlier motion to consider it with the Hitchcock Reservations was also defeated. The Senate then adjourned until the new session began in December.

Were the Lodge Reservations so crippling that Wilson was justified in spurning them even at the cost of defeating the Treaty? A number of historians have concluded that although most of the reservations were redundant, unnecessary, and even petty in tone, they left the Covenant essentially intact and would not have seriously interfered with the functioning of the League. Wilson's obduracy, therefore, has been attributed to the effects of his illness and to the bitterness of his personal relations with Senator Lodge. These factors can be easily exaggerated. The illness no doubt rendered the president more suspicious and irritable than before and it did isolate him for a period from public opinion and the political currents within the Senate. Yet by November he had recovered enough to confer with Hitchcock,

---

[7] Lansing to Polk, November 17, 1919, The Papers of Frank L. Polk, Yale University Library.

and subsequently with others, and to resume a measure of his duties. His militant opposition to strong reservations before his stroke suggests that even if he had not experienced the illness his attitude would not have materially changed. His dislike of Lodge undoubtedly did make him more resistant to the reservations, but it probably was not the most important factor behind his actions. Wilson sincerely believed that the reservations were so unsound that rejection of the Treaty was preferable if it could not be approved in any other way.

Many of the Lodge proposals were obviously directed at Wilson personally and violated his concept of the proper function of the legislative and the executive branches of government. The effect of such reservations as the first one, which accorded Congress the power of withdrawal from the League by concurrent resolution, would have been to deprive the president of all voice in certain areas of foreign policy since a concurrent resolution is not subject to presidential approval. Wilson saw this as an impermissible effort to usurp presidential responsibilities in foreign affairs. He opposed the preamble because its requirement for the specific assent of the other major powers might force renegotiation of the entire Treaty or cause other states to try to enter the League with objectionable reservations.

Wilson particularly was distressed by the second reservation relating to Article X. He viewed the collective guarantee as the very heart of the League and felt that any weakening of its provisions would wreck the entire structure. There was no need for a qualification in any case as he had repeatedly said on his western tour. The obligation of Article X was a moral one only; no action was automatically provided by the article and the United States would be protected by its veto power in the League Council, the enforcement organ of the League, and by the obvious requirement under the Constitution for congressional authorization to declare war, appropriate money, and increase the military establishment. To enter the League with this reservation, in Wilson's view, would be dishonorable and even cowardly; it would be to ask special treatment as a member. The basic difference between entering the League of Nations with or without the Lodge Reservations was the very significant difference between a limited and grudging participation in world affairs, and Wilson's concept of an America willingly assuming the full burdens of a great power and becoming actively involved in making the League a success. Nothing less than the latter would satisfy his vision of the new America.

The defeat of the Treaty in the Senate shocked many citizens and led to an increased demand for a compromise. It seemed incredible to supporters of the League that an overwhelming majority of senators claimed to favor participation in the League of Nations and yet were unable to agree on the form of ratification. Delegations called upon both Lodge and Hitchcock to urge approval of the Treaty, and Wilson was requested to accept it with reservations if necessary in order to get the League into operation. There were also indications that the major European states preferred the United States to enter the League with reservations rather than risk remaining outside. In early March French Ambassador Jules Jusserand discussed the problem with officials in the State Department and suggested such a solution to the problem.

The British government initially had great doubts about the acceptability of the reservations, but it too seems eventually to have agreed that the participation of the United States in the League was essential even if it could be obtained only through the Lodge formula. A memorandum by a crown legal adviser to the British Foreign Office, sent to Washington for the guidance of the ambassador-designate, Viscount Grey of Fallodon, agreed that President Wilson was probably correct in concluding that the reservation relating to Article X removed the heart of the Covenant and would weaken the confidence of smaller powers in the League. It would have the effect of forcing Great Britain to assume most of the burden of enforcing collective security. Other reservations were also found objectionable, especially the one directed against the six votes of the British Empire in the League Assembly. The Foreign Office informed Grey, on November 27, that the admission of the United States on a different basis from other states would endanger the very existence of the League: "Indeed we very much doubt whether it will be possible to admit the United States to the League with any reservation having an external effect without automatically breaking down the Covenant." [8] General Smuts took a less serious view of the reservations and advised that American membership was so vital that the United States should be allowed to enter even on the basis of rather unreasonable terms. Ambassador Grey concurred although he was more disturbed than Smuts by the reservations. By early 1920 Prime Minister Lloyd George apparently also had reached that conclusion. When Grey returned to England at the end of 1919, he published a letter in *The Times* of London which discussed the necessity of American membership and concluded that even the problem caused by the reservation on the six votes of the empire probably could be resolved by amicable negotiation. His letter was regarded in America as indicative of official British attitudes and strengthened Lodge in his reservation strategy.

Wilson refused to retreat. Since Lodge also was unwilling or unable to compromise, the result was the final rejection of the Treaty by the Senate. When the Treaty came before the Senate for the last time, the preamble to the attached reservations had been made slightly less objectionable by the deletion of the requirement for the specific assent to the changes by the other powers, but a fifteenth reservation was attached in behalf of Irish freedom. In a letter to Senator Hitchcock, on March 18, President Wilson in effect again requested Democratic solons to vote against the Treaty with the reservations. When the vote came on March 19, 1920, the Treaty with the reservations fell short of the necessary two-thirds majority by seven votes, receiving forty-nine for to thirty-five against. Twenty-three Democrats, in obedience to Wilson's wishes, voted with the Irreconcilables against the Treaty, whereas twenty-one joined Lodge and the Republican reservationists in its support. Obviously both sides were guilty of playing politics. The Republicans had used the reservations, at least in part, for political gain and to humiliate Wilson. Just as clearly, many Democrats had viewed entry into the League with the reservations as preferable to not entering at all, which was the only practical choice, and yet from loyalty to

---

[8] E. L. Woodward and R. Butler, eds., *Documents on British Foreign Policy, 1919-1939*, First Series (London: His Majesty's Stationery Office, 1947-1958, 12 vols.), V, 1040-1042.

the president had voted against the Lodge Reservations. Even if the Treaty had passed, however, there can be little doubt but that the grimly determined president would have rejected it with the reservations.

V

Still confident that he would eventually succeed, President Wilson briefly considered requesting a popular vote of confidence on the League issue. He thus revealed his penchant for the parliamentary system, toward which he thought the United States was slowly evolving, and his failure to grasp the popular mood favoring compromise. His plan was to challenge by name some fifty-seven senators to resign their posts and to seek immediate reelection. If they were replaced by pro-League men, Wilson would have achieved his goal, but if a majority of the challenged senators were reelected he proposed to appoint a Republican as secretary of state and then, with the cooperation of the vice-president, to resign the presidency to that person. The plan has been condemned as preposterous by some historians and it was definitely out of keeping with past American practices. But granted Wilson's belief in the tendency toward a parliamentary system, in which he proved to have been a poor prophet, it was a carefully conceived scheme for coping with the deadlock in the Senate. Further reflection and advice from the attorney-general persuaded the president to put it aside. Not all of the challenged senators would have obliged him by resigning and in a number of states the necessary special elections were constitutionally impossible.

The embattled but uncompromising president then turned to the idea of converting the 1920 election into a popular referendum on the question of League membership without any qualifications. He had announced the plan in a public letter to the Democrats assembled for the annual Jackson Day Dinner on January 8, 1920. In this public letter Wilson again branded the proposed Lodge Reservations as completely unacceptable and he requested that the next election be "a great and solemn refer-

endum, a referendum as to the part the United States is to play"
in the preservation of world peace.[9] Apparently Wilson, despite
his poor health, seriously considered departing from the Jeffer-
sonian tradition to seek a third term in office as the best means
of highlighting the key issue in the proposed referendum. Bain-
bridge Colby, who had succeeded Lansing as secretary of state
in early 1920, went to the Democratic national convention at
San Francisco and maneuvered for Wilson's renomination. Colby
was persuaded to abandon the effort by other members of the
administration who, because of their personal loyalty and affec-
tion for the president, realized that renomination would be the
equivalent of a death sentence for him.

Governor James M. Cox of Ohio finally emerged with the
Democratic nomination. He and his vice-presidential running
mate, Franklin D. Roosevelt, supported membership in the
League and agreed to accept reservations which did not seriously
impair the Covenant. The Republican nominee, Senator Warren
G. Harding of Ohio, was less clear on the subject. The tenor of
his remarks, which varied considerably during the campaign,
could be interpreted as either favoring the League with changes
which would make it safe for America, the devising of an entirely
new league, or as an indication of hostility to any league. After
the Irreconcilables indicated great displeasure with his straddling
techniques, Harding in subsequent speeches condemned Wilson's
League as totally bad and declared that he did not want to clarify
the Covenant but to repudiate it. At the same time, he tried to
assuage pro-League Republicans by promising that as president
he would work for a new association of nations, presumably
based on a world court and arbitration machinery. A committee
of thirty-one prominent pro-League Republicans then issued a
declaration that the Republican Party would take the United
States into a league of nations. The motive apparently was to
prevent Harding, virtually assured of victory in the election, from
following an isolationist course in office. Although Cox identified his candidacy with the need to continue progressivism and
to avoid domestic reaction, in the last weeks of the campaign he

---

[9] *Congressional Record*, 66th Congress, 2d Session, Vol. 59, 1249.

particularly emphasized the league issue. It was a question, he asserted, of the present League or none at all, and not of some vague new plan.

The nature of American presidential elections prevents them from providing a meaningful popular mandate on any single issue, particularly a complicated one such as membership in the League. Personalities, traditional loyalties, and a variety of domestic issues and grievances tended to overshadow the League question in the 1920 campaign. The prevailing sentiment among a majority of voters evidently was one of general discontent with Wilsonism, whatever the particular grievance might be, and a demand for a change in the national government. Yet when Harding overwhelmed his Democratic opponent by a margin of nearly seven million votes, he and his Republican advisers interpreted it as a popular mandate against membership in the League. In office, therefore, he failed to act on the promised new association of nations. Possibly a majority of citizens still favored participation in the League with reservations designed to protect American interests. By his insistence on a "solemn referendum" when he should have known the near impossibility of such a decision under the American political system, Wilson helped make virtually inevitable Harding's subsequent interpretation of the meaning of the election.

Many factors entered into the rejection of the Treaty. Not all Americans were willing to break with the past and its comfortable isolationist traditions. An even larger number, probably a majority of the citizenry active in public affairs, was aware that isolationism was no longer possible and that the nation must play a larger role in foreign affairs in keeping with its power, interests, and responsibilities. But the transition from isolationism to internationalism had been so rapid and bewildering that many reasonable and conscientious people hoped that America's involvement at least initially could be more limited and gradual. These supported League membership but wanted some safeguards incorporated which would curtail the degree of American commitment and responsibility. To President Wilson, however, nothing less than unqualified participation in the League was worthy of America and would ensure the success of the organization. It seems clear that he deliberately chose to keep the nation out, at least for a time, rather than enter the League of Nations with the Lodge Reservations. Wilson himself, a dedicated internationalist, thus contributed to the disillusionment and isolationism which characterized the postwar decade.

The Wilsonian advocates of internationalism lost, but not completely or permanently. It proved impossible in the 1920's to return to the pre-1914 American role in foreign affairs. Too much had happened, too many connections and threads were left from the war for that to be feasible. There were large foreign war debts to negotiate and collect; separate treaties of peace to arrange with Germany, Austria, and Hungary; some degree of interest in the functioning of the mandate system, especially in the biblical lands of the Near East; the threat of a great naval arms race to be avoided and problems in the disturbed Far East to settle; and the existing League and many of its activities, particularly in the areas of disarmament and nonpolitical enterprises, were of great interest to the United States. Above all, many thoughtful Americans could not forget the sacrifices in lives and money caused by American involvement in the war and remained resolved in the future to avoid the mistakes of the past in rejecting League membership. A pattern emerged described by Selig Adler as the new isolationism, the middle-road approach of the 1920's between the older isolationism and Wilsonian internationalism. World War I marked a great departure for the United States from the less-demanding world of the past and into the more dangerous but challenging world of the twentieth century.

Suggestions for Additional Reading

THERE IS NO adequate study of American foreign policy for the entire period of World War I from 1914 to 1920. The brief account by Charles Seymour, *Woodrow Wilson and the World War* (New Haven, 1921), was written before official and private papers were open to scholars. General accounts of both domestic and foreign events are offered by Frederick L. Paxson, *American Democracy and the World War* (Boston, 1936, 3 vols.), and Preston W. Slosson, *The Great Crusade and After: 1914–1928* (New York, 1931). William E. Leuchtenburg, *The Perils of Prosperity, 1914–32* (Chicago, 1958), briefly surveys the period in several perceptive chapters, and Robert E. Osgood, *Ideals and Self-Interest in America's Foreign Policy* (Chicago, 1953), devotes approximately one-third of his study to the Wilson era.

President Wilson has been the subject of numerous biographies and studies which cover in whole or in part the foreign policies of his administration. The volumes by Ray Stannard Baker are rich in documentary materials although uneven in narrative and analytical treatment: *Woodrow Wilson: Life and Letters* (Garden City, N.Y., 1935–1939, 8 vols.), and *Woodrow Wilson and World Settlement* (Garden City, N.Y., 1922, 3 vols.). An interpretative study by Harley Notter, *The Origins of the Foreign Policy of Woodrow Wilson* (Baltimore, 1937), is still of value. H. C. F. Bell, *Woodrow Wilson and the People* (Garden City, N.Y., 1945), is an older but sound one-volume biography. Arthur S. Link is in the process of completing a definitive multi-volume study of Wilson and his era: *Woodrow Wilson and the Progressive Era, 1910–1917* (New York, 1954), covers both domestic and foreign affairs in the neutrality period; *Wilson: The Struggle for Neutrality, 1914–1915* (Princeton, 1960) is a detailed study of the formative period in the shaping of American neutrality; *Wilson: Confusions and Crises, 1915–1916* (Princeton, 1964), carries the account through the *Sussex* crisis; and *Wilson the Diplomatist, A Look at His Major Foreign Policies* (Baltimore, 1957), consists of a series of stimulating essays on Wilson's role in the diplomacy and peacemaking of World War I. Also see his *Woodrow Wilson: A Brief Biography* (Cleveland and New York, 1963). John M. Blum, *Woodrow Wilson and the Politics of Morality* (Boston, 1956); and John A. Garraty, *Woodrow Wilson, A Great Life in Brief* (New York, 1956), are excellent short studies of the man and his times. The Garraty book contains some interesting psychological insights into Wilson's personality. A. L. and J. L. George, *Woodrow Wilson and Colonel House* (New York, 1956), have utilized theoretical concepts from dynamic psychology to interpret persuasively the interaction between Wilson's personality and his political actions. The second volume of Arthur Walworth's rather adulatory *Woodrow Wilson* (New York, 1958, 2 vols.), covers the diplomacy of the Wilson era. The 1956 centennial of Wilson's birth occasioned an outpouring of special studies. The essays on Wilsonian foreign policy in Em Bowles Alsop, ed., *The Greatness of Woodrow Wilson* (New York, 1956); Edward H. Buehrig, ed., *Wilson's Foreign Policy in Perspective* (Bloomington, Ind., 1957); Arthur P. Dudden, ed., *Woodrow Wilson and the World of Today* (Philadelphia, 1957); and Earl Latham, ed., *The Philosophy and Politics of Woodrow Wilson* (Chicago, 1958), contain valuable comments by well-known scholars. Herbert Hoover's *The Ordeal of Woodrow Wilson* (New York, 1958) focuses on Hoover's personal views on the events of the period. An excellent guide to recent Wilsonian literature is found in Richard L. Watson, Jr., "Woodrow Wilson and His Interpreters, 1947–1957," *Mississippi Valley Historical Review*, XLIV (1957), 207–236.

The role of Wilson's principal adviser is related in Charles Seymour, *The Intimate Papers of Colonel House* (Boston, 1926–1928, 4 vols.), part documentary and part biography. Bryan has not yet received a good full study, but the following works which examine aspects of his career are valuable: Paul W. Glad, *The Trumpet Soundeth; William Jennings Bryan and His Democracy, 1896–1912* (Lincoln, 1960), is useful for background on Bryan's youth and personality; Merle E. Curti, *Bryan and World Peace* (Northampton, Mass.: Smith College Studies in History, 1931), examines his plans and efforts to promote new approaches to peace; J. V. Fuller's older sketch, "William Jennings Bryan" in S. F. Bemis, ed., *The American Secretaries of State and Their Diplomacy* (New York, 1929), X, 5–44, should be supplemented by Richard Challener, "William Jennings Bryan, 1913–1915" in Norman A. Graebner, ed., *An Uncertain Tradition: American Secretaries of State in the Twentieth Century* (New York, 1961), 79–100. Challener depicts Bryan as representing a dated provincialism in foreign as well as domestic affairs. Julius W. Pratt's "Robert Lansing" in Bemis, *American Secretaries of State,* (1929), X, 47–175, is a still useful treatment of Wilson's second secretary of state. For a shorter sketch, consult Daniel M. Smith, "Robert Lansing, 1915–1920" in Graebner, *An Uncertain Tradition,* 101–127.

The causes of American intervention in the European war have been the subject of much historical debate. An excellent guide to the pertinent literature is provided in an essay by Richard W. Leopold, "The Problem of American Intervention, 1917: An Historical Retrospect," *World Politics,* II (1950), 405–425. C. Hartley Grattan, *Why We Fought* (New York, 1929), is an early scholarly work which sought to revise the official and standard explanation of America's entry into the war and to attribute it instead to the unneutrality of the Wilson policies. Walter Millis, *Road to War: America, 1914–1917* (Boston, 1935), is a critical and satirical account which emphasizes newspapers and public opinion. Edwin Borchard and W. P. Lage, *Neutrality for the United States* (New Haven, 1937), and Alice M. Morrissey, *The American Defense of Neutral Rights, 1914–1917* (Cambridge, 1939), are also censorious of American policies and interpretations of international law. The latest "revisionist" study, *America Goes to War* (Boston, 1938), by Charles C. Tansill, is a well-researched volume which is sharply condemnatory of the pro-Ally attitudes of Wilson, House, and Lansing. War with Germany is attributed primarily to the economic and diplomatic unneutrality of the United States. Most scholars, however, have found more convincing the interpretations advanced by Charles Seymour in *American*

Diplomacy During the World War (Baltimore, 1934), a survey of the neutrality period and the diplomacy of the war to the signing of the armistice in 1918, and *American Neutrality, 1914–1917* (New Haven, 1935). The latter book consists of a series of essays countering the charges of the revisionists and maintaining that the defense of neutral lives and rights against the submarine menace alone explains the entry of America into the war. In recent years several studies have appeared which reappraise the neutrality period within the larger context of economic, psychological, and political developments both in the United States and in the principal European belligerent countries. Edward H. Buehrig, *Woodrow Wilson and the Balance of Power* (Bloomington, Ind., 1955), reevaluates the roles of House and Lansing, and portrays Wilson as aware of balance of power or national security considerations but as moving beyond these ideas to the concept of collective security as best for the peace of America and the world. Daniel M. Smith, *Robert Lansing and American Neutrality, 1914–1917* (Berkeley, 1958), emphasizes the realistic element in Lansing's thought and policies. An excellent study of the evolution of German policy toward the United States is provided by Karl E. Birnbaum, *Peace Moves and U-Boat Warfare* (Stockholm, 1958). Ernest R. May's *The World War and American Isolation, 1914–1917* (Cambridge, 1959), is an important multi-archival work which analyzes the diplomatic controversies of the neutrality years within the context of domestic politics in Great Britain, Germany, and the United States. *The British Press and Wilsonian Neutrality* (Stanford, 1951) by Armin Rappaport is a good study of the reactions of the British public to American policy. Link's volumes, previously cited, also add new perspectives to an understanding of the problems of neutrality. Marion C. Siney, "British Negotiations with American Meat Packers, 1915–1917: A Study of Belligerent Trade Controls," *Journal of Modern History*, XXIII (1951), 343–353, and *The Allied Blockade of Germany, 1914–1916* (Ann Arbor, 1957, a projected 2-volume study) are good on Allied maritime policy toward the neutrals. Also see Edgar Turlington, *The World War Period*, Vol. III, in P. C. Jessup et al., *Neutrality, Its History, Economics and Law* (New York, 1936, 3 vols.); and

R. G. Albion and J. B. Pope, *Sea Lanes in Wartime* (New York, 1942). Belligerent propaganda is examined in James Duane Squires, *British Propaganda at Home and in the United States from 1914 to 1917* (Cambridge, 1935); H. C. Peterson, *Propaganda for War, the Campaign Against American Neutrality, 1914–1917* (Norman, Okla., 1939); and James M. Read, *Atrocity Propaganda, 1914–1919* (New Haven, 1941). For studies of public opinion, see the following: Carl Wittke, *German-Americans and the World War* (Columbus, Ohio, 1936), and C. J. Child, *The German-American in Politics, 1914–1917* (Madison, Wisc., 1939), examine the impact of the war on that group in the United States; Edwin Costrell, *How Maine Viewed the War, 1914–1917* (Orono, Me., 1940), J. C. Crighton, *Missouri and the World War, 1914–1917* (Columbia, Mo., 1947), Cedric Cummings, *Indian Public Opinion and the World War, 1914–1917* (Indianapolis, 1945), are good state studies with implications for other areas of the country; and Samuel R. Spencer, Jr., *Decision for War, 1917* (Rindge, N. H., 1953), and Barbara W. Tuchman, *The Zimmermann Telegram* (New York, 1958), emphasize the impact of the *Laconia* sinking and the Zimmermann telegram in America's transition into war in early 1917.

Aspects of American wartime diplomacy, in addition to the previously cited study by Seymour, are covered by Thomas A. Bailey, *The Policy of the United States toward the Neutrals, 1917–1918* (Baltimore, 1942); David F. Trask, *The United States in the Supreme War Council* (Middletown, Conn., 1961); and Arthur Willert, *The Road to Safety, A Study in Anglo-American Relations* (London, 1952). Louis L. Gerson, *Woodrow Wilson and the Rebirth of Poland, 1914–1920* (New Haven, 1953), attributes great effect to the influence of Polish-American groups on Wilson's attitude toward the restoration of Poland. Victor S. Mamatey, *The United States and East Central Europe, 1914–1918* (Princeton, 1957), praises Lansing for being first among American leaders to favor the emergence of the succession states and denies that the Balkanization of Europe can be primarily attributed to Wilson's peace program. Ruhl J. Bartlett, *The League to Enforce Peace* (Chapel Hill, 1944), traces the emergence of that citizen movement and its educational campaign for collective security. Lawrence E. Gelfand, *The Inquiry:*

American Preparations for Peace, 1917–1919 (New Haven, 1963), presents a careful analysis of the organization, functions, and influence of the scholars assembled under the general supervision of House to plan for the peace treaty. The reciprocal influence of Wilson and British advocates of a liberal peace is detailed by Laurence W. Martin, *Peace Without Victory: Woodrow Wilson and the British Liberals* (New Haven, 1958). A. J. Mayer, *Political Origins of the New Diplomacy, 1917–1918* (New Haven, 1959); and John L. Snell, "Wilson's Peace Program and German Socialism, January-March, 1918," *Mississippi Valley Historical Review*, XXXVIII (1951), 187–214, and "Wilsonian Rhetoric Goes to War," *The Historian*, XIV (1952), 191–208, evaluate the impact of Wilson's Fourteen Points and other addresses on belligerent war aims and public opinion. Two articles by Claude E. Fike examine aspects of the decision to intervene in Russia and Wilson's desire to preserve Russian integrity: "The Influence of the Creel Committee and the American Red Cross on Russian-American Relations, 1917–1919," *Journal of Modern History*, XXXI (1959), 93–109; and "The United States and Russian Territorial Problems, 1917–1920," *The Historian*, XXIV (1962), 331–346. William A. Williams, *American-Russian Relations, 1781–1947* (New York, 1952), describes American participation in the Siberian intervention as basically anti-Bolshevik in character, in constrast to Betty Miller Unterberger, *America's Siberian Expedition: 1918–1920* (Durham, N. C., 1956), who depicts Wilson as reluctantly consenting in order to restrain unilateral Japanese expansion. George F. Kennan's exhaustively researched and detailed study, *Soviet-American Relations, 1917–1920:* Vol. I, *Russia Leaves the War* (Princeton, 1956), and Vol. II, *The Decision to Intervene* (Princeton, 1958), credits Lansing with a major role in formulating the policy of nonrecognition of the Bolshevik regime and stresses the rescue of the Czechoslovak legion as a prime cause of the Siberian intervention. Christopher Lasch, "American Intervention in Siberia: A Reinterpretation," *Political Science Quarterly*, LXXVII (1962), 205–223, concurs that the basic factor behind the intervention was military necessity related to rescue of the Czechs and the halting of German activities. For American reactions to the 1917 Russian revolutions, see Lasch, *The American Liberals and the Russian Revolution* (New York, 1962); and Leonid I. Strakhovsky, *American Opinion about Russia, 1917–1920* (Toronto, 1961). Pauline Tompkins, *American-Russian Relations in the Far East* (New York, 1949), is a good general study; and Strakhovsky's *The Origins of American Intervention in North Russia, 1918* (Princeton, 1937), covers the other Russian venture of the United States. For the motives of America's collaborators in intervention, consult James William Morley, *The Japanese Thrust into Siberia, 1918* (New York, 1957); and Richard H. Ullman, *Anglo-Soviet Relations, 1917–1921: Intervention and the War* (Princeton, 1961). H. R. Rudin's *Armistice, 1918* (New Haven, 1944) is the standard study of the negotiations leading to the German capitulation.

The most detailed account of the peace negotiations is in Harold W. V. Temperley, *A History of the Peace Conference of Paris* (London, 1920–1926, 6 vols.), based on the limited number of memoirs and printed documents then available. For two of the more controversial accounts by participants, see John Maynard Keynes, *The Economic Consequences of the Peace* (New York, 1920); and Harold Nicolson, *Peacemaking, 1919* (Boston, 1933). Paul Birdsall, *Versailles Twenty Years After* (New York, 1941), is the most detailed one-volume study of the entire conference. He denies that the peace treaty was Carthaginian and credits Wilson with statesmanlike efforts. Thomas A. Bailey, *Woodrow Wilson and the Lost Peace* (New York, 1944), is critical of Wilson's rigidity and stubbornness at Paris but acknowledges his devotion and zeal in the cause; the treaty is seen as better for Wilson's presence and efforts, with most of the Fourteen Points realized in the settlement. An excellent recent study which throws much light on the essential harmony between American and British peace aims is found in *Anglo-American Relations at the Paris Peace Conference of 1919* (Princeton, 1961) by Seth P. Tillman. Among the more specialized works on the conference, consult F. S. Marston, *The Peace Conference of 1919, Organization and Procedures* (London and New York, 1944); René Albrecht-Carrié, *Italy at the Paris Peace Conference* (New York, 1938); Ivo J. Lederer, *Yugoslavia at the Paris Peace Conference* (New

Haven, 1963); and Sherman D. Spector, *Rumania at the Paris Peace Conference* (New York, 1962). Focused on the American role are P. M. Burnett, *Reparations at the Paris Peace Conference from the Standpoint of the American Delegation* (New York, 1940, 2 vols.); and Louis A. R. Yates, *The United States and French Security, 1917–1921* (New York, 1957). George Curry, "Woodrow Wilson, Jan Smuts, and the Versailles Settlement," *American Historical Review*, LXVI (1961), 968–986, details the influence of Smuts on Wilson's league plans. Kurt Wimer, "Woodrow Wilson's Plan to Enter the League of Nations through an Executive Agreement," *Western Political Quarterly*, XI (1958), 800–812, explains heretofore puzzling aspects about Wilson's plans for a preliminary peace during the early stages of the conference. Robert H. Ferrell, "Woodrow Wilson and Open Diplomacy," in G. L. Anderson, ed., *Issues and Conflicts: Studies in Twentieth Century American Diplomacy* (Lawrence, Kans., 1959), relates one of Wilson's Fourteen Points to his subsequent conduct at Paris. George F. Kennan details the Russian problem at the conference in a section of his study, *Russia and the West under Lenin and Stalin* (Boston, 1961). The Shantung question and its background is covered briefly in A. W. Griswold, *The Far Eastern Policy of the United States* (New York, 1938); and more extensively in Roy Watson Curry, *Woodrow Wilson and Far Eastern Policy, 1913–1921* (New York, 1957). Also see Tien-yi Li, *Woodrow Wilson's China Policy, 1913–1917* (New Haven, 1952); and R. H. Fifield, *Woodrow Wilson and the Far East: the Diplomacy of the Shantung Question* (New York, 1952). Fifield views Lansing, House, and the other American advisers as having only a small influence on Wilson's solution to the problem. An excellent study of Lansing's Far Eastern diplomacy which throws new light on the Lansing-Ishii Agreement is found in Burton F. Beers, *Vain Endeavor, Robert Lansing's Attempts to End the American-Japanese Rivalry* (Durham, N. C., 1962). Also see his earlier article, "Robert Lansing's Proposed Bargain with Japan," *Pacific Historical Review*, XXVI (1957), 391–400. For works on other members of the American peace commission, see Allan Nevins, *Henry White, Thirty Years of American Diplomacy* (New York, 1930); and Frederick Palmer, *Bliss, Peacemaker;*

the Life and Letters of General Tasker H. Bliss (New York, 1934).

T. A. Bailey examines the defeat of the treaty in the United States in an excellent interpretative study, *Woodrow Wilson and the Great Betrayal* (New York, 1945). He attributes primary responsibility for the defeat to Wilson more than to Lodge. An important work by Selig Adler, *The Isolationist Impulse, Its Twentieth Century Reaction* (New York, 1957), emphasizes the significance in the debate over the treaty of the liberal defection from the Wilson coalition and concludes that a majority of Americans were not psychologically ready for a vigorous course of internationalism. Also see Alan Cranston, *The Killing of the Peace* (New York, 1945); D. F. Fleming, *The United States and the League of Nations, 1918–1920* (New York, 1932); and Chapter 10 in W. Stull Holt, *Treaties Defeated by the Senate* (Baltimore, 1933). The motives of the leader of the Senate opposition are examined by John A. Garraty, *Henry Cabot Lodge: A Biography* (New York, 1953). For studies of other Republicans involved in the League fight, see P. C. Jessup, *Elihu Root* (New York, 1938, 2 vols.); Richard W. Leopold, *Elihu Root and the Conservative Tradition* (Boston, 1954); Belle C. and Fola La Follette, *Robert M. La Follette* (New York, 1953, 2 vols.); Henry F. Pringle, *Life and Times of William Howard Taft* (New York, 1939, 2 vols.); and Marion C. McKenna, *Borah* (Ann Arbor, 1961). More specialized topics are covered by R. W. Logan, *The Senate and the Versailles Mandate System* (Washington, 1945); and C. C. Tansill, *America and the Fight for Irish Freedom* (New York, 1957). Wilson's speaking tour and health are examined by Dexter Perkins, "Woodrow Wilson's Tour" in Daniel Aaron, ed., *America in Crisis* (New York, 1952), 425–465; and Rudolph Marx, *The Health of the Presidents* (New York, 1960). Daniel M. Smith, "Robert Lansing and the Wilson Interregnum, 1919–1920," *The Historian*, XXI (1959), 135–161, discusses Lansing's unsuccessful effort to solve the problem of Wilson's disability. Three articles by Kurt Wimer examine Wilson's efforts to secure Senate approval for an unmodified Treaty: "Woodrow Wilson's Plan for a Vote of Confidence," *Pennsylvania History*, XXVIII (1961), 279–293; "Woodrow Wilson and a Third Nomination," *ibid.*,

XXIX (1962), 193–211; and "Woodrow Wilson Tries Conciliation: An Effort that Failed," *The Historian*, XXV (1963), 419–
438. Wesley Bagby, *The Road to Normalcy: the Presidential
Campaign and Election of 1920* (Baltimore, 1962), describes the
election as an unusually decisive one which answered negatively
the questions of whether the United States should continue on
a progressive and internationalist course.

Index